Dave

BLITZ OVER SUSSEX 1941- 42

Pat Burgess
Andy Saunders

MP Middleton Press

Cover pictures-

Left. Dismembered wreckage of a Heinkel 111 was scattered across Smokehouse Farm, Shipley, on 13th March, 1941, where it was shot down by a nightfighter. Here, a wing section has come to rest against farm buildings.

Right. Two Army Officers in this car had a miraculous escape when bombs hit Victoria Drive, Bognor Regis, on 16th December, 1942. The resident of the shattered house, however, was killed, as was another civilian nearby. The German bomber responsible was shot down onto Bognor Gasworks.

May the sacrifices made by those airmen in the service of their respective countries and the scale of civilian loss of life resulting from aerial warfare over the county not be quickly or carelessly forgotten. This book is a tribute to all who suffered.
ANDY SAUNDERS & PAT BURGESS

First published October 1994

ISBN 1 873793 35 9

© Middleton Press 1994

Design - Deborah Goodridge

Published by Middleton Press
            Easebourne Lane
            Midhurst
            West Sussex
            GU29 9AZ
            Tel: (0730) 813169
(From 16 April 1995 - (01730) 813169)

Printed & bound by Biddles Ltd,
            Guildford and Kings Lynn

CONTENTS

Map of the administrative boundaries effective in 1940 and used throughout this book. The figures are the page numbers, listed above.

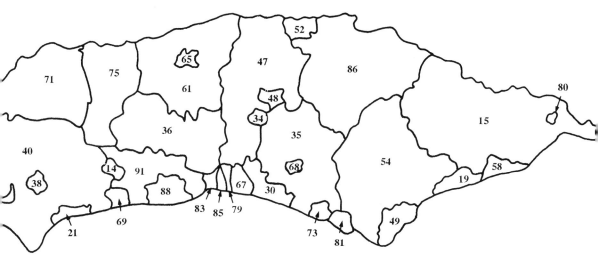

English Channel

ACKNOWLEDGEMENTS

Our thanks goes to those who have generously given their time and knowledge or who have helped with the supply of photographs for this book. In particular, Peter Foote, Steve Hall, Flt.Lt. Chris Goss, Michael Payne, Martin O'Brien, Simon Muggleton, Len Smith, Joyce Warren, Nancy Woodall, Freda Mitchell, Jeff West, Ron Gammage, Terry Connolly, Cliff White, Bob Elliston, Simon Parry, Dr.Rod Oakland, Margaret Bird (Rye Museum), Victoria Williams (Hastings Museum), David Dunstall, Tony Rogers, Jim Croft, David C.Milton, Denis Cullum, Reg Randell, Gordon Ramsey, Winston Ramsey, Roger Freeman and Ian Hutton.

Thanks also to Vic Mitchell for support and encouragement in getting this book and collection of photographs together.

Thanks also goes to staff at the East and West Sussex Country Records Offices, the Evening Argus, Bexhill-on-Sea Observer, Hastings & St. Leonards Observer, Kent & Sussex Courier, West Sussex Gazette, Mid Sussex County Times and Chichester Observer.

Thanks go to Brian Bridges for his helpful input to the project over several years and to Trevor Linford for his hard work in preparing the text and captions.

A special mention must also go to Mrs. Jenny Hickman, daughter of the Bognor Regis photographer, Mr.Frank Lalouette, for making available her late fathers superb collection without which this book would have been difficult to produce. Last, but no means least, to Julie and Barbara for putting up with our work on this project.

AUTHORS NOTES

Following the success of our previous volume, "Battle Over Sussex - 1940", there was clearly a demand for books in the same format and covering the county for the remainder of the war period. This, then, is the first of two volumes which will cover 1941 to 1945. "Blitz Over Sussex, 1941 - 42", looks at the period when the country braced itself in the face of the German "Blitz" against Britain. This was a period when Sussex was still reeling from the trauma and excitement of the Battle of Britain in 1940, and when its people faced new dangers and difficulties. Night attacks and "Hit and Run" raids on coastal towns were very much a feature of the years 1941 and 1942, but from the Spring of 1941 the German war machine turned its attention eastwards on the Soviet Union. This resulted in something of a downturn in German air activity over the British Isles due to the fact that a majority of front line units were transferred to the Eastern Front, leaving what was almost only a token force on the Channel Coast. This reduction in air activity by the German side is reflected in the correspondingly reduced number of German losses over Sussex and the markedly fewer British aircraft being brought down through air combat in skies directly above the county. On the other hand, the RAF was first starting to go seriously onto the offensive over Europe, and there were therefore an increasing number of RAF aircraft coming down in Sussex after returning damaged or low on fuel from missions over the continent. Also, from 1942 the involvement of the Americans in the war would lead to an increasing number of aircraft of the USAAF coming down in Sussex.

In this book, however, we have not only looked at the aspect of aircraft related incidents but have attempted to paint a much broader picture of wartime events as they affected Sussex. Hopefully, this approach will give something of a flavour of the times for those who were not there - and plenty of nostalgia and reminiscences for those who were! It is not intended, however, that this book should be a comprehensive and exhaustive record of all wartime events in the county. Instead, we have drawn out certain notable or significant events and incidents in a district by district basis. In doing this the boundaries of rural districts, urban districts, municipal boroughs and county boroughs then in being have been used.

Documentary materials from official archives, contemporary records, eye witness accounts and from a variety of other sources have all been used in the compilation of this book. Similarly, the wide range of pictures used have come from an equally wide range of

4

sources, although it has not been possible to find pictures relating to all the administrative areas in the county.

The authors would be delighted to hear from anyone with new information, photographs or souvenirs relating to the war in Sussex. They may be contacted via Tangmere Military Aviation Museum, Tangmere Airfield, Chichester, West Sussex. PO20 6ES.

MAPS

The maps are all based upon the 1940 edition of the Ordnance Survey of Great Britain. Four regions of the county have been selected to give a representative coverage of East and West Sussex on which have been marked a proportion of the aircraft down in those areas. For clarity, not every aeroplane down in each area covered by these maps has necessarily been marked. Those that have been marked are indicated in the exact position if known, or at a close proximation to the believed or reported position of the crash. The size of the county and number of incidents logged precludes the inclusion of maps for the whole of the county marked with the many incidents on record. The scale has been reduced to 0.75" to 1 mile. The numbers shown on the maps are listed in the tables on pages 93 - 95.

PHOTOGRAPHS

Every effort has been made to clear copyright but the sources of pictures used are varied and, in many cases, obscure. Some are from private collections and others from agencies and organisations no longer in existence. Therefore, the publication of any picture for which clearance has not been given is unintentional. It is hoped, however, that their appearance within this book will be seen as a tribute to civilians and service personnel who died or suffered in the county of Sussex during the period 1941 to 1942.

RAF ORGANISATION

Whilst the organisation of RAF operational units into Squadrons will no doubt be familiar to most readers, it is perhaps worth explaining that each Squadron comprised roughly about twelve aircraft and a corresponding number of pilots or aircrew. Clearly this number was subject to fluctuation depending upon serviceable aircraft and losses of pilots or machines. A Squadron could often be depleted to below strength pending the replacement of men or machines. However, the Battle Order of the RAF can be found elsewhere in other reference works, although it is worth mentioning here that the entire County of Sussex fell within the defence region of No. 11 Group, RAF Fighter Command.

LUFTWAFFE ORGANISATION

The organisation of the German airforce and the official designation of its operational units will not be familiar to many readers and thus a brief explanation of such designations as used within the context of this book is appropriate.

German operational units were divided up into Geschwaders; a Geschwaders translating roughly into English as Squadron. However, the strength of a Geschwader was many times that of a Squadron, but it was sub-divided up into tactical units which more closely represented the strength of an RAF Squadron. Fighter units were Jagdgeschwaders (abbreviated to JG) and Bomber units were Kampfgeschwaders (abbreviated to KG). Within each Geschwader there could be up to five groups (Gruppen), each sub-divided up again into Staffeln, the nearest approximation to an RAF Squadron. Additionally, each Gruppe had its Staff Flight (Stab) of H.Q. Staff.

RAF AND LUFTWAFFE RANK EQUIVALENTS

Aircraftman (2)	(AC2)	(Fl)	Flieger
" (1)	(AC1)	(Gefr)	Gefreiter
Leading Aircraftmen	(LAC)	(Obgefr)	Obergefreiter
Corporal	(Cpl)		Hauptgefreiter
Sergeant	(Sgt)	(Uffz)	Unteroffizier/Unterfeldwebel
Flight Sergeant	(Flt Sgt)	(Fw)	Feldwebel
Warrant Officer	(WO)	(Oberfw)	Oberfeldwebel/Stabsfeldwebel
Pilot Officer	(Plt Off)	(Lt)	Leutnant
Flying Officer	(Fg Off)	(Oblt)	Oberleutnant
Flight Lieutenant	(Flt Lt)	(Hptm)	Hauptmann
Squadron Leader	(Sqn Ldr)		Major
Wing Commander	(Wg Cdr)		Oberstleutnant
Group Captain	(Gp Capt)		Oberst

The above is a list of approximate equivalents in rank of the two services although the opposites are necessarily speculative in some cases as no exact equivalent may always exist. In brackets the abbreviated version of the rank as used in this book is given as appropriate.

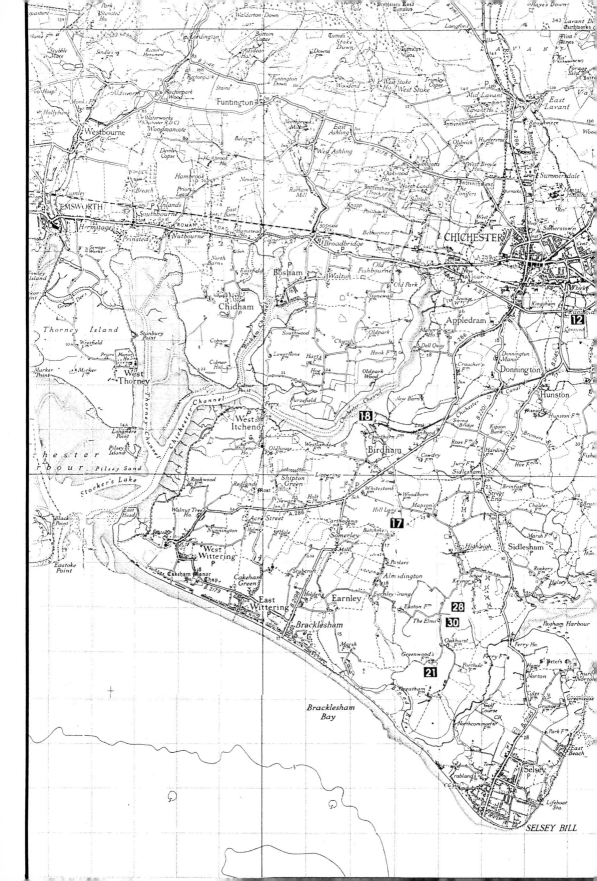

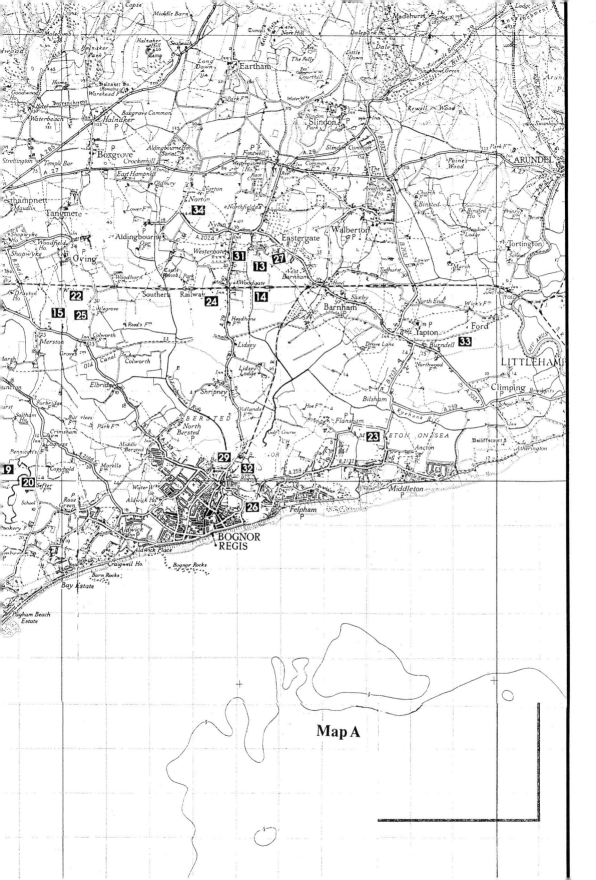

Map A

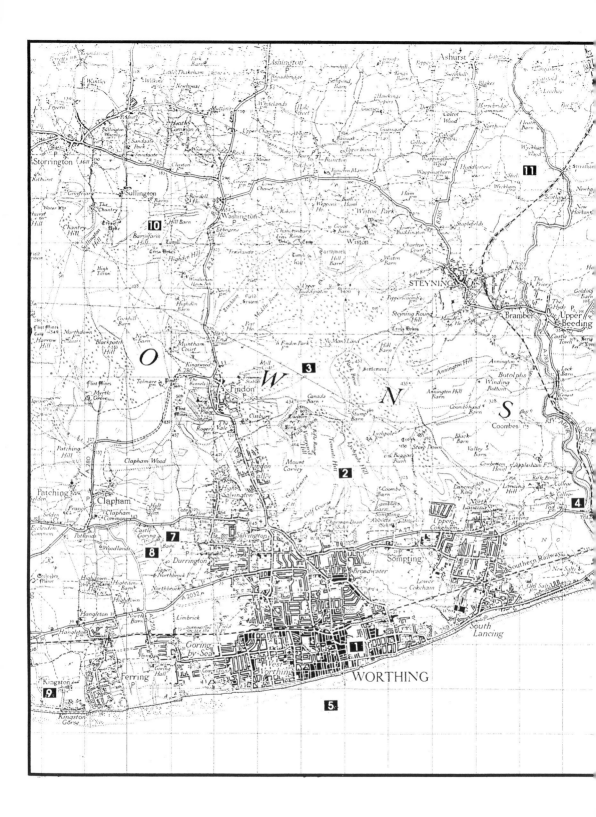

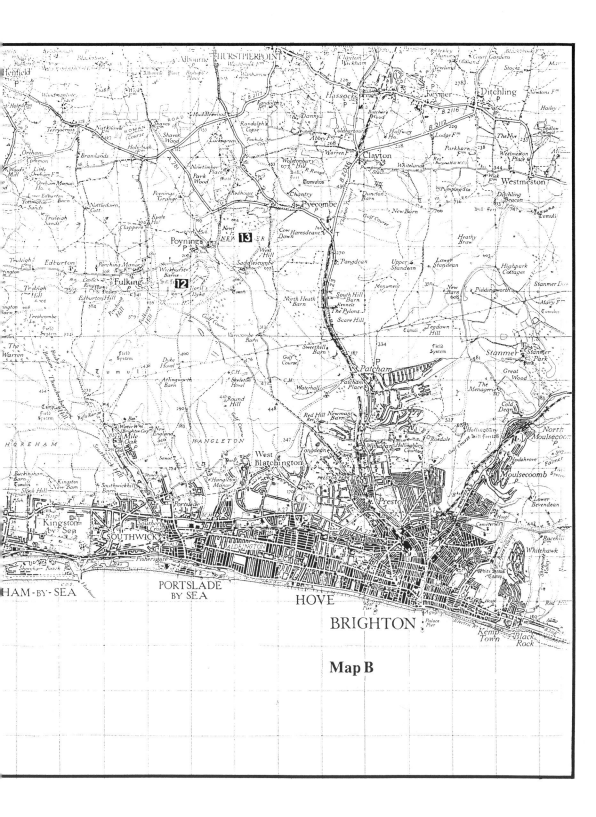

Map B

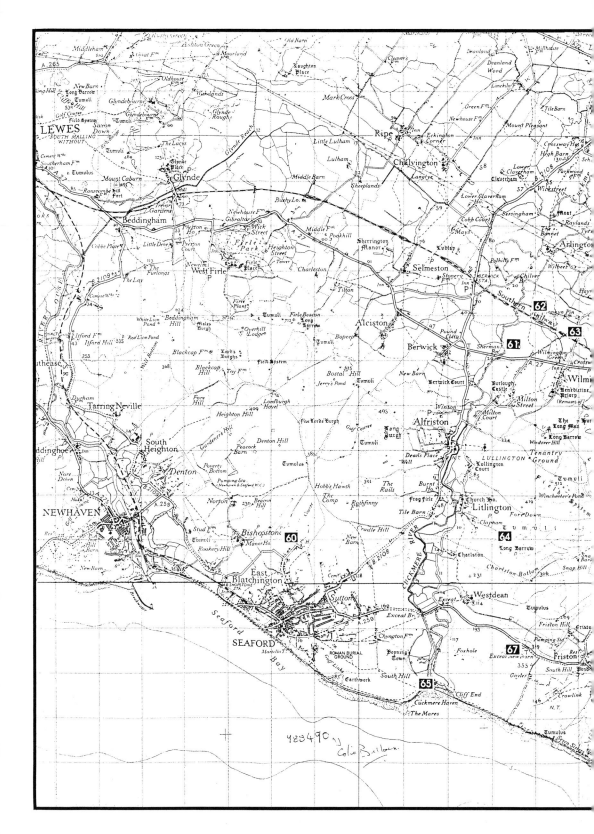

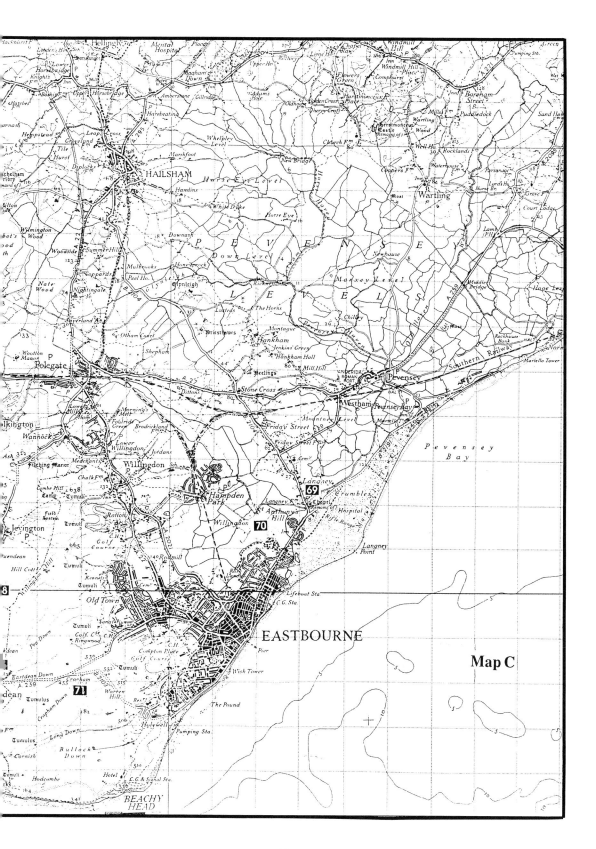

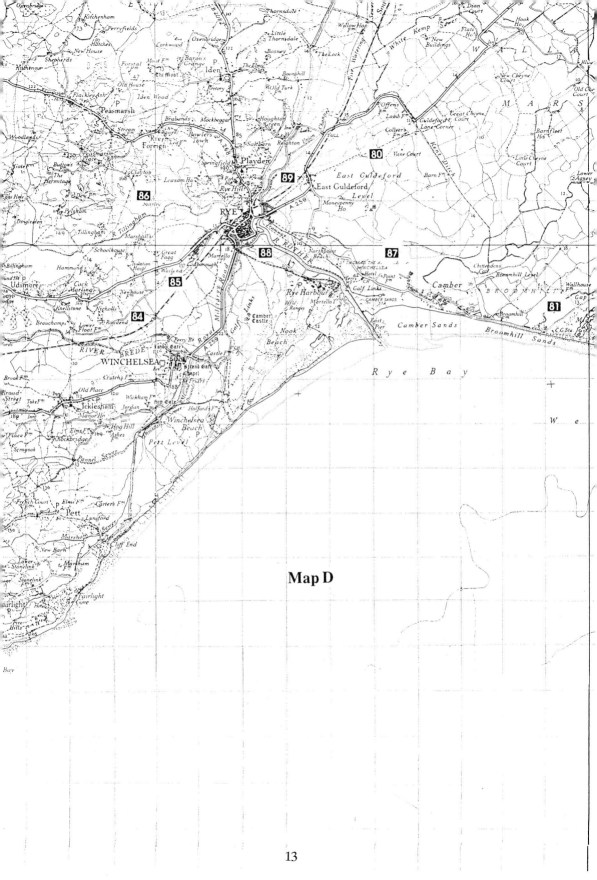

Map D

ARUNDEL MUNICIPAL BOROUGH

The official record confirms that, by great good fortune, no civilian casualties were inflicted upon the population of the Arundel Municipal Borough during the entire duration of the war. That is not to say, however, that the Borough did not see its moments of excitement and drama and, in common with other South East towns, it experienced a fair share of military activity and air raid warnings. Aerial battles often raged overhead. It was, though, spared the horror of any significant air raid but numerous bombs are recorded as having fallen in the district. For example on the night of 2nd May, 1941, five high explosive bombs were dropped to the east of London Road causing slight damage to the roof of Green Lodge, Arundel Park, but no casualties. Most likely the bombs were simply jettisoned by a returning raider unable to find its target or else engaged or damaged by British defences and thus eager to shed its load. A huge tonnage of bombs were scattered across the county in this random fashion, very often aimed at no specific target and, thankfully, often causing minimal damage and casualties

On 5th August, 1942, two Spitfires of 412 Squadron collided in mid air with both falling at Priory Farm, killing the pilots - P/O Koell-hoffer and Flt. Sgt. Luxton. Within a few weeks another tragic accident claimed the lives of a further two RAF airmen when a General Aircraft Owlet spun into the ground at Warningcamp Farm with the loss of Pilot Officers Jordan and Dunphy. The aeroplane was a trainer based at Ford with 605 Squadron, and used for the purpose of training pilots on the techniques of landing "tricycle" undercarriage aircraft like the Douglas Boston with which the Squadron was equipped. The diminutive Owlet was a one-off, being the only one of its kind ever built. The RAF roundels on its crumpled wreckage were used as rifle practice targets by the Canadian soldiers who guarded the wreck- an ignominious end for such an unusual aeroplane.

On the 24th of the following month a Hurricane crashed into Rewell Wood killing its pilot, and not far away 2nd Lt. Ward of the USAAF became one of the first American casualties in the county when his Westhampnett based Spitfire broke up in a dive and crashed near Whiteways Lodge. In the space of three months the Borough had seen five Allied fatalities - all of them caused by accident rather than through air combat.

1. This unusual aeroplane, a General Aircraft Owlet, was the only one of its type ever built and was lost with its two occupants in a crash at Warningcamp Farm on 30th August, 1942.

BATTLE RURAL DISTRICT

Covering a large part of East Sussex the high proportion of crashed aircraft, bombing incidents etc. experienced in the region during 1940 continued on into the years 1941 and 1942 although the decrease in aerial battles from 1940 translated into a corresponding decrease in the number of aircraft losses through combat. Even so, a total of at least sixteen aeroplanes, Allied and Enemy, are recorded as down in the district during this period.

The first enemy aircraft brought down in the area since 1940 was a Messerschmitt 109 shot down at Blackhouse Farm, Camber, on 24th April, 1941, by Biggin Hill based Spitfires of 92 Squadron. The pilot, Oberfeldwebel Gunther Struck, released a bomb in the direction of Rye Railway Station before baling out into captivity. His Messerschmitt, meanwhile, plunged into the soft marshy soil at Blackhouse Farm, Camber, and buried itself deeply on impact. It was recovered in a 1974 excavation.

On 14th June a Heinkel 111 was shot down by a night fighter at Lower Snailham Farm, Doleham, and jettisoned its cargo of 200 incendiary bombs across an adjacent field before its pilot, Oberfeldwebel Paul Wiersbitzky, made a forced landing suffering no more than minor cuts. His three crew members had baled out unhurt, but an unfortunate cow, caught in the rain of incendiary bombs, was killed.

The most extraordinary German aircraft loss, however, involved that of a Dornier 217 which landed intact at Jury's Gap, Camber, on 12th October, 1941, becoming the first example of this type of aircraft to fall into the hands of the RAF. Its capture was due to false radio-location beacons operated by the RAF which, transmitting decoy signals, caused the crew to lose their bearing and when totally lost, forced them to land as their fuel ran low. The pilot, Oberleutuant Dolenga, had concluded he was over Northern France but was utterly confused when he saw a coastline to the south. He must have been bewildered when met by British soldiers!

Thankfully, civilian casualties were light during 1941 with only the death of Home Guardsman James Cantle, 63, recorded as being "Due to Enemy Action" on 19th March, 1941, at The Bungalow, Blacklands, Crowhurst.

With the further decline in enemy activity over the country during 1942 all of the aircraft losses recorded during the year in this district were of Allied machines. Most notable was the Photo Reconnaissance Spitfire which dived into the banks of a tributary of the river Brede near Winchelsea Railway Station on 24th April, 1942, burying itself deep in the soft alluvial soil and taking with it the body of its unfortunate pilot, 20 year old Pilot Officer Charles Barber. For decades the family had sought to have him recovered for a decent Christian burial but were told by the authorities that this was impossible. Then, in 1986, the aircraft was recovered from a depth of over 30ft in a difficult operation by the Tangmere Military Aviation Museum at the request of the Barber family. Finally, later that year, Charles Barber was laid to rest with full Military honours near his Doncaster home.

On 19th August, 1942, the Dieppe Raid involved huge air support from the Royal Air Force, and, for the first time, included Britain's new American Allies. One of the Spitfires of the all American "Eagle Squadron", returning damaged from Dieppe, reached Burwash before Pilot Officer Julian Osborne was forced to bale-out. Over the following years many of his fellow countryman would add to statistics of those killed or injured on active service within the county.

It was not only those in the air or on the ground who suffered. Therefore we should not forget those who were in peril on the seas off our coastline. For example, fishermen Charles Hollands and Walter Longly both died when their fishing boat "Mizpah" was machine gunned by the dreaded Focke Wulf 190s off Icklesham, on 16th September, 1942. The skipper of the "Mizpah", Charlie Locke, was injured in the attack and subsequently awarded the BEM. This, after all, was total war and everyone was in the front line. Fishermen, farmers, shop workers, civilians and children were as much on the receiving end of enemy bombs and bullets as were soldiers, sailors and airmen and no less than twenty four innocent civilians were killed in Battle Rural District Area by enemy action during the war - the oldest 84, the youngest just days old.

➤

Defending the civilian population were airman of many nations and on 23rd October, 1942, a young Belgian, Pilot Officer Raymond Dopere, died when his Typhoon - one of the RAF's latest fighters - crashed and burnt out at Ashburnham. Raymond had suffered greatly in his efforts to reach Britain and continue the fight against Germany but was denied ever seeing the fruits of victory and the liberation of his homeland which he had helped achieve.

The tragedy which claimed his life was simply caused by flying into high ground when returning from patrol in bad weather.

As the year drew to a close, an incident at Rye Foreign which was apparently a machine - gun attack, claimed the life of 39 year old George Shilling from Maidstone who succumbed to his wounds at Rye Memorial Hospital later that same day, 11th December, 1942.

2. The swastika marked tailfin of Oberfeldwebel Gunther Struck's Messerschmitt 109 is uncovered from 10ft of marshy soil at Blackhouse Farm, Camber, during 1974. It was shot down on 24th April, 1941, Struck having baled out into captivity.

Women's Land Army:

EAST SUSSEX

NAME Miss F. R. Relf

No. 156927.

You are now employed
in the

.........WADHURST.........District
and
.the ~~District Organiser~~
~~Committee Member~~
who is responsible
for you is

...Miss Tindall,...............

Castle Place, Lewes,.........

Tel.   .....Lewes 673~4.......

If you want any help or
advice
you should immediately
write or telephone to
her.

3. Unteroffizier Herbert Schick was one of the crew members of a Heinkel 111 taken prisoner on 14th June, 1941, when shot down at night on Lower Snailham Farm, Doleham.

4. On 12th October, 1941, this Dornier 217 became the first aircraft of its type to fall into RAF hands when it landed almost intact at Jury's Gap, Camber. Its radio navigation equipment had been confused by British countermeasures and the crew became lost, being forced to land when short of fuel.

5. Oberleutnant Dolenga was captain of the Jury's Gap Dornier. On board the aeroplane was a bottle of champagne to be drunk on completion of the mission to celebrate Dolenga's birthday. Presumably it went unopened by the German crew!

6. Pilot Officer Charles Bertram Barber was the pilot of a Spitfire which crashed near Winchelsea Railway Station on 24th April, 1942 his remains were found in the wreckage of his aeroplane during 1986 he was subsequently buried with full military honours in accordance with his family's wishes.

BEXHILL MUNICIPAL BOROUGH

Although a small Borough, its coastal position ensured there was excitement and drama enough for this otherwise rather genteel and retiring Sussex town, but thankfully the fairly serious bombing of parts of the town experienced in 1940 was not repeated. However, the Borough Accountant's Office, forced to abandon its Town Hall offices through bomb damage in 1940, had re-located at 23 Sutherland Avenue - only to be bombed yet again on 8th April, 1941, when the building was partly burnt out in an incendiary attack. On 23rd July, 1941, a Spitfire of 610 Squadron made a forced landing on the outskirts of the town at Constables Farm, Little Common; its pilot, Sgt Philpotts, safe. Another Spitfire crashed in rather more dramatic circumstances just off Bexhill sea front on 27th September, 1941, after the RAF had encountered the Luftwaffe's devastating new fighter, the Focke Wulf 190, for the very first time. Damaged, the aeroplane had descended to 800ft before Sgt. Jeff West, DFM, a New Zealander, had escaped by parachute at the last moment. He was rescued from the sea - shaken but unhurt - by local fishermen Mr. J. Easton and Mr. F. Hunisett who rowed out to collect him. Over fifty years later parts of the Spitfire are still washed up onto Bexhill beach, and in recent years a commemorative plaque, mounted with part of the Spitfire, has been sent out to Jeff West at his New Zealand home.

Bombs returned to Bexhill with a vengeance again on 9th May, 1942, with a daylight low-level raid by four fighter bombers sweeping in at wave top height, dumping their high explosives and destroying Longly Bros shop in Devonshire Road, the "Bexhill Observer" offices next door, St. Barnabas' Vicarage in Brassey Road, Sackville Garage in Middlesex Road, and the last bomb falling near to the Golf course. Miraculously, there were no causalities in any of these incidents. The next edition of the "Bexhill Observer", restricted by wartime censorship, recorded only that a "South Coast Town" had been raided - but of course all the readers knew exactly which town it was. Theirs!

Retribution, though, was to come on 2nd September, 1942, when a Focke Wulf 190 was shot down into the sea off Galley Hill by a Spitfire of 401 Squadron, it's pilot Unteroffizier von Jutrzenka being rescued by launch and taken prisoner.

Fortunately, during the period covered by this book there were no civilian fatalities in the town and the population, anxious to bolster efforts to end the war, collected a magnificent £176,000 during the "War Weapons Week" of 1941 and an equally impressive £224,468 during the 1942 "Warship Week". The year ended, though, with a sad reminder of the human price still being paid by local service personnel when Sgt. Robert Harrison, RAF(VR), was buried with Full Military Honours in the Turkey Road Cemetery after being killed on active service on 5th December, 1942.

8. Recovered in the 1980s, this relic of Jeff West's Spitfire was presented to the former pilot at his New Zealand home.

7. Sgt. Pilot Jeff West, lying on top of the Spitfire engine, was pilot of a Spitfire shot down into the sea off Bexhill on 27th September, 1941, and who was rescued by local fishermen.

9. This was the scene in Devonshire Road, Bexhill, after fighter bombers had struck on 9th May, 1942.

BOGNOR REGIS URBAN DISTRICT

With RAF Tangmere on one side and Ford Aerodrome on the other it was inevitable that Bognor Regis would get it's fair share of aerial activity - not to mention bombings and the other trials and dramas which the unusual conditions of war time brought.

At the very height of the night Blitz, on 11th April, 1941, random bombs claimed at least two lives - although Home Office reports indicate there were three fatalities. Only Elsie Cripps and Albert Holloway, a Fire Guard, can be identified as casualties from the Civilian War Dead Roll - Elsie dying from her injuries in hospital whilst Albert died in an incident at Havelock Road. That same day Winston Churchill had spoken of Britains civilians amongst the ruins with " .... the spirit of an unconquerable people." The part which Albert Holloway played as Fire Guard epitomised in some small way that spirit, as the nation's civilian population stood shoulder to shoulder in the face of unparalled danger.

A double tragedy struck Spitfires of the Tangmere Fighter Wing when, on the 21st July, 1941, one aircraft of 616 Squadron crashed on approach to Tangmere at Oldlands Farm, Shripney, killing Sgt. Pilot Nelson. Shortly afterwards a Spitfire of 145 Squadron spun into the ground at Marigolds Field, Shripney, killing Sgt. Pilot Gilbert as he searched for the crash site of Nelson's aeroplane. It was just one of wars tragic misfortunes. In November, on the 23rd, another Spitfire was lost - this time an aircraft of 41 Squadron which came down in the sea off Bognor.

On the 14th April, 1942, a Hampden bomber of 144 Squadron came to grief at Sea Road, Felpham, after returning from operations. The aeroplane crashed and burnt out killing its crew and causing some local consternation when an unexploded bomb was discovered in the white-hot burning metal of the bomber. Fortunately it did not explode.

On the 14th August, 1942, the town suffered a significant number of casualties in the bombing of the Sudley Road area. In total, there were some eight fatalities. Just over a month later, on the 7th September, the bombers returned again - this time causing two fatalities at Goodman Drive.

On the 26th February, 1942, a deranged Canadian Soldier, Pte. John Moore, shot dead Police Sgt. William Avis after escaping from Military custody and being cornered in Fernhurst Gardens. Making good his escape he managed to reach South Mimms in Hertfordshire before being captured. He was finally committed for trial at the Old Bailey on a charge of murder. He was clearly mentally unbalanced and, indeed, found to be insane and incapable of standing trial. Whilst this was an extreme case, incidents involving Servicemen in violent, criminal or anti-social acts were by no means uncommon and certain conscripted troops had an almost fearsome reputation!

Noteworthy is the part played in recording local events around the Bognor area by photographer Frank Lalouette, whose pictures have been used extensively in this publication. Throughout the war he produced a series of photographs of remarkable clarity and detail which provide a valuable insight into events of the times.

One incident recorded by Mr.Lalouette was the dramatic episode on the 16th December, 1942, when a Beaufighter of 141 Squadron chased a Dornier 217 at low level across the town and caused it to crash into a gasometer at Bognor Gas Works. Unexploded bombs were scattered in and around the gasometer, along with wreckage of the aeroplane and the bodies of all four crewman. The loss of an enemy aircraft was always a boost for civilian morale, although this episode resulted in the deaths of two civilians; Harold Booker, 65, and Georgina Hepton, 26, both losing their lives in the town on this day. However, although the war had yet to run another two and a half years the town was spared the misery of any further significant civilian casualties - only two more fatalities being recorded in Bognor Regis for the remainder of the war years.

10. By 1941 the threat of invasion had receded, but Council workmen still toiled long hours making concrete tank traps, or "Dragons' Teeth" as they were called. Here, the Duke of Gloucester and military VIPs inspect the defences at Bognor Regis.

11. Bren Carriers trundle through Bognor Regis as part of a parade to mark War Weapons Week in March, 1941. The Mayor and other dignitaries take the salute from the Arcade entrance.

12. Sgt. Pilot Frederick Nelson of 616 Squadron, Tangmere, was killed when his Spitfire crashed at Oldlands Farm, Shripney, on 21st July, 1941.

13. Children at War. This cherubic figure sits astride a British 250 lb G.P. bomb at Bognor during the 1941 War Weapons Week. The bomb has been liberally plastered with war savings stamps.

14. Women at war. Female NFS Messengers on their motorcycles at Bognor Fire Station. The headlamp masks were required to meet black-out regulations.

15. Police Sgt. William Avis, murdered in Fernhurst Gardens, Bognor Regis, by a deranged Canadian Army deserter, Private John Moore.

16. Burnham Avenue was also hit on 14th August, 1942. Here, dazed inhabitants, servicemen and rescuers emerge as the dust begins to settle.

17. Further down Burnham Avenue a woman delivering bread had a remarkable escape when she hid beneath this handcart as a bomb cratered the road just yards away. Here, an ARP Warden checks off his casualty list.

18. When bombs hit the town on 14th August, 1942, this huge crater tore Sudley Road apart and killed eight people.

19. Rescue workers tear at the rubble in Sudley Road to free victims and to search, hopefully, for survivors.

20. Mill House in Marine Drive West, Bognor, took a direct hit on 17th September, 1942. Firemen survey the rubble.

21. Bognor Gasworks was a regular target for attack and was hit no less than seven times. Once, on 16th December, 1942, a crippled Dornier actually flew into one of the gasholders and crashed. Here, the aftermath of an attack by Messerschmitt 109's is shown on 3rd July, 1942. The gasholders were punctured and set alight and Mr W.R. Hammond (left) and Mr H. Glazier (centre) seal the leaks with wet clay. Mr Hammond received the MBE and Mr Glazier the BEM for this work.

22. On another occasion a bomb passed through the gasholder on the right (see gashed side) and exploded on a mined bridge over Aldingbourne Rife, Shripney. The date was 17th September, 1942.

23. This was all that remained of the bridge following the blast which also severed gas, water and electricity services.

BRIGHTON COUNTY BOROUGH

One of the town's worst raids took place during the night of 8th/9th April, 1941, when the Blitz on London and other major cities was in full swing. Bombs rained down onto the residential area of Norfolk Square, causing massive damage, killing at least ten and injuring many more - including a woman and her six year old daughter who were dug out alive from under a collapsed building after sixty hours!

Airborne over Sussex throughout the Blitz period were the Beaufighters of 219 Squadron from Tangmere, patrolling and intercepting night raiders with considerable success. Tragedy, however, befell the Squadron on 30th April, 1941, when two of its aircraft collided over the town. Only Sgt. Twidale escaped by parachute, Sgt. Forster, Pilot Officer Black and Pilot Officer Holman all losing their lives. Just over two months later there was retribution of sorts when a Heinkel 111 bomber was shot down into the Channel off Brighton, three of the four crew being rescued and taken prisoner. Before the end of the year, however, 219 Squadron suffered yet another loss when one of its Beaufighters went down in the sea off the town after its port engine failed.

In the Autumn of 1941, not long after the formation of the National Fire Service, the NFS College was established in the Ocean Hotel, Saltdean, being opened by the Home Secretary, Mr. Herbert Morrison. Holiday-makers had long forsaken the area and the empty Hotel lent itself for conversion to a training college - even the unused swimming pool coming in handy for pump drill!

On the night of the 8th May, 1942, 219 Squadron were able to avenge their own losses with the destruction of a Heinkel 111 at Ewes Bottom, Patcham, when Squadron Leader Topham, DFC, and Flying Officer Berridge shot the aircraft down in a spectacular and dramatic fashion. Hitting the enemy aircraft from astern with a burst of cannon and machine gun fire the Beaufighter crew saw a "...terrific flash". The aircraft was on fire and going down and Berridge and Topham then saw the wreckage burning on the ground. As it hit, a series of brilliant blue flashes arced out in a long line across the countryside North of Brighton as high tension cables were hit by the falling debris. Ironically, the power cut it caused blacked out - momentarily - the Wartling GCI Radar Site which had helped control the fighter onto its quarry. When morning came wreckage was found strewn far and wide from the impact point with the complete tail unit the only recognisable part of the Heinkel left. Its unfortunate crew of five were smashed to pieces across the farmland. More than fifty years on and tiny pieces of the bomber still turn up in the fields and adjacent hedgerows. The five Germans, were buried in the town's Bear Road Cemetery.

Inevitably photographs of shot down enemy machines provided excellent propaganda, but so too did bombing incidents which affected hospitals, schools etc. Therefore, when bombs fell on the St. Annes Home for Crippled Children in Buckingham Place on 12th October, 1942, the newspapers made much of this "...Nazi Frightfulness." In the incident two year old Anthony Leadbeater was killed and his death added to the propaganda value of the raid in which several other children were also injured. Elsewhere throughout the Borough there were other casualties and fatalities on this day, and raids such as this were now a regular feature as hit-and-run attacks against coastal towns became commonplace. On the 18th December bombs hit Rottingdean, severely damaging The Vicarage and St. Margarets Flats and fatally injuring War Reserve Constable Harold Stone of the Brighton Police.

After more than two years of war the lives of the civilian population had been in ever increasing turmoil and the upheaval was felt no more keenly than by the residents of Stanmer where twenty dwellings, a shop and the Church had to be evacuated during 1942 to make way for a military training area. The hundred or so inhabitants had quite expected that invasion in 1940 would render them homeless - but now they were being dispossessed by their own side! Such were the sacrifices that Britain's civilian population were asked to make in support of the war effort.

24. On 30th April, 1941, two Beaufighters of 219 Squadron collided over Brighton, killing three aircrew. Here, the fliers of 219 Squadron are pictured at RAF Tangmere. 219 Squadron played a major part in the story of the air war over the county of Sussex.

25. A Miles Magister aircraft at Tangmere in 1942. It was in an aircraft of this type that Mr. George Martin, Secretary to the Mayor of Brighton, was killed whilst being given a flight during a Mayoral visit to RAF Tangmere. The Magister crashed near Tangmere, killing both the pilot and Mr. Martin.

26. This was the aftermath of the destruction on 8th May, 1942, of a Heinkel 111 at Patcham. Only the battered tail section was left relatively intact.

27. Memorial card printed for the family of 25 year old Wilhelm Markl, one of the crew members who died in the crash at Patcham on 8th May, 1942.

28. The local haulage firm, Nicholls & Co, were contracted to the Air Ministry for the collection and removal of wrecked aircraft across Southern England. Exhibits were also conveyed to "War Weapons Week" displays in 1941. Here, two employees of Nicholls & Co. pose with a de-activated SC 1800 "Satan" bomb. Perhaps a reader will be able to identify the location?

Chriſtliches Andenken

an Herrn

Wilhelm Markl

Unteroffizier und Bordfunker in einem
Kampfgeſchwader, Inhaber des Eiſernen
Kreuzes 2. Kl.

der bei einem Nachteinſatz ge-
gen England im Mai 1942 im
25. Lebensjahre, in treuer
Pflichterfüllung für Volk und
Heimat gefallen iſt.

Herr gib ihm die ewige Ruhe,
laſſ' ihn ruhen in Frieden!

Mein Jeſus Barmherzigkeit!

Druck: H. Zauner Lambach

29. Also in Patcham during May, 1942, this UXB was dealt with in the garden of a house at Highview Avenue.

30. Much propaganda value was found in the bombing raid on Brighton which hit St. Anne's Home for Crippled Children, Buckingham Place, on 12th October, 1942, killing a two year old boy. This was the aftermath.

31. Unexploded mines were often washed ashore on the Sussex coast, and Brighton beach was no exception. A German mine washed up on 11th December, 1942, was secured to the groynes by ropes before being dealt with by the Naval bomb and mine disposal experts of HMS Vernon.

BURGESS HILL URBAN DISTRICT

Although the wail of the air raid siren frequently rose and fell over the District, records show that air raid incidents were few and far between. In total, only about fourteen high explosive bombs and two hundred incendiaries fell in the area and there were no fatalities or casualties. Indeed, no premises were destroyed by enemy action, only two were damaged seriously but capable of repair and only forty one were slightly damaged. By comparison with other areas in the region, these figures are remarkably low. Nevertheless, there were 1,056 air raid alerts and one of those lasted for nearly fourteen hours - although local rumour had it that this was only because someone forgot to sound the "All-Clear"!

The war did not entirely pass the District by, however, and saw two military casualties being buried with full military honours during the period covered by this book. The first was Sgt. Peter Warner, of 56th Bn. Reconnaissance Corps, who died on 1st April, 1941, and the other was 2nd Lt. Alan Bagot, 70th Bn. Kings Royal Rifle Corps, who died on 29th August, 1942. Their graves are at St. John's and St. Andrew's Churchyard's respectively.

Meanwhile, aerial activity continued overhead throughout 1941 and 1942 with Allied aircraft and enemy raiders passing to and fro. No aircraft were brought down in the District during this period, however.

32. Burgess Hill escaped any serious air raid incidents. Perhaps its inhabitants maintained a good blackout?

CHAILEY RURAL DISTRICT

Like its neighbour, Burgess Hill, the Rural District of Chailey - encompassing some twenty seven Parishes - was remarkably fortunate in the comparatively few casualties or fatalities it suffered through enemy air attacks. Nevertheless, activity by the Luftwaffe was by no means a rare event and, on 31st January, 1941, a Heinkel 111 bomber crashed at Wales Farm, Plumpton, in the late afternoon. Low flying in the gathering gloom and bad visibility the bomber flew into anti-glider landing poles, crashed, and burnt out. All five crew perished on what is now part of the Plumpton Agricultural College. Its intended target London, was spared the load of four 500Kg bombs - although at the time of the crash only three bombs from its main load were discovered amongst the wreckage. The mystery of the fourth bomb was not solved until 1993, when it was accidentally unearthed just below the surface of the field with groove marks made over the years by countless plough shares in its steel fins! Rendered harmless by a bomb disposal team the bomb is now displayed in the Agricultural College.

At Newick, on 27th May, 1941, bombs at The Lodge, Lower Birchlands, killed 62 year old Percy Horsley and injured a Mrs. Ford, Miss Bannister and a boy, Cyril Holman. Other than this sad incident, German attacks were minimal. However, shortly before the bombing which killed Percy Horsley, the "Bismarck" was being sunk many miles away in the Atlantic with the loss of over 2,000 lives. That was warfare on an entirely different scale - but all the same, Percy Horsley was one of 60,000 civilian fatalities suffered in the United Kingdom. This was a war that was killing men in their thousands, as on the "Bismarck", and in ones or twos in isolated villages and hamlets like Newick. The barbarism of this war affected everyone - whoever they were and whatever they were.

Early in 1942 Air Ministry surveyors arrived at Bower Farm and Great Homewood Farm, Chailey, to map out a new RAF airstrip known as an Advanced Landing Ground or ALG.

Although not opened until 1943, this was part of the massive run-up to D-Day. The need to create forward air bases along the South Coast to operate the massive aerial armada an invasion would require gave rise to several of these ALG's in Sussex

Perhaps, had the ALG been completed, it could have provided a safe haven for the Spitfire of 72 Squadron which crashed not far away at Sedlow Wood, Westmeston, after engine problems forced Sgt. Robertson to abandon his aeroplane by parachute on 14th March. The stricken Spitfire plunged into the Sussex clay, from where the Wealden Aviation Archaeological Group recovered the siezed Rolls Royce Merlin during the early 1970s.

Not so lucky was fellow Spitfire pilot Sgt. Barton of 605 Squadron who lost his life as his aircraft smashed into Stanford Buildings, West Firle, on 22nd May, and with such awful ferocity that a good portion of the substantial brick and flint dwelling was demolished. One civilian was injured and 25 others had to be evacuated.

A little under a month later, on 19th August, the sky over Sussex had been thick with Allied aircraft heading out to the beachhead of the Dieppe raid to become embroiled in what was, at the time, the biggest single air battle in history. Many returning aircraft were damaged stragglers seeking a safe haven; one was the Spitfire of Sgt. Raeder of 322 (Norwegian) Squadron whose aeroplane had been severely damaged by a Focke Wulf 190 and only made it as far as The Brooks, Rodmell, before crash landing.

This was the last aeroplane down in the District during the period covered by this book, and for some while the scale of the aerial war seemed to diminish so far as it affected the people of Chailey Rural District. But, as we shall see in the next volume, there was more to come. Things were far from over, and this had only been the end of the beginning! Nevertheless, although they could not know it, they were to be spared any further civilian casualties for the remainder of the war.

33. This was the 500Kg bomb discovered at Plumpton Agricultural College in March, 1994 - a lethal legacy of the crash on 31st January, 1941, of a Heinkel 111 bomber. It was made safe by an RAF bomb disposal team and is seen here with College Chief Executive, John Wilson.

CHANCTONBURY RURAL DISTRICT

As with Chailey, the casualties here were light - three civilian deaths being recorded throughout the wars duration and none of them within the period covered by this book.

On the 19th January, 1941, however, a Heinkel 111 crashed in flames and smashed itself to pieces across the fields of Wyckham Farm, Steyning, with no hope of survival for its crew of five. The reasons for the crash are obscure, although there are indications it may have been hit by anti-aircraft fire over Shoreham. Its pilot, Hauptmann Graf zu Castell, radioed his ground control station in France with a final message "Starboard engine on fire, landing in England". Moments later the aeroplane was a flaming wreck, with only the heat blistered tail section left to identify this as a Heinkel. All five crew members were laid to rest in Steyning Churchyard.

In February, on the 20th, a Hurricane of 302 (Polish) Squadron crashed during dogfight practice over the Arundel District and dived vertically into the ground at Rackham killing outright its young Polish pilot, Pilot Officer Edward Pilch. The fighter was smashed to pieces, the majority of the wreckage being driven deep underground by the force of the impact.

Another sad loss was that on 10th March, 1941, when Sgt. Ben Bingley of 616 Squadron was killed when his Spitfire smashed into the ground through unexplained reasons at Wiston. Writing to Ben's family, his CO, Squadron Leader Burton explained: *"He was ordered up with two other aircraft to investigate a raid out to sea. They were crossing the coast near Worthing at about 21,000 ft when the Section Leader - F/Lt Holden - saw your son, who was flying No.3. in formation, lagging a long way behind. He called Sgt. Bingley on the radio but got no reply. From details we have received from eye witnesses it appears that shortly after this your son's aircraft went into a steep dive and carried on until it hit the ground. He was killed instantaneously. The exact cause of the accident is very difficult to ascertain, but my personal view is that he did not allow himself enough oxygen."*

Ben Bingley, a 24 year old Hospital Administrator from Leicester, was laid to rest in St. Andrew's Churchyard, Tangmere. As will be seen from this volume, the rate of attrition to the Royal Air Force through accident was exceedingly high and many more lives were lost over Sussex through misadventure than combat.

Although the scale of air activity by the enemy was decreasing noticeably into 1942, it is fact that the war was hardly going well for the Allies at this time. Thus, with the great victory achieved at El-Alamein, there was at last cause for some celebration and on Sunday, November 15th, the Government directed that church bells be rung to celebrate the event. For over two years the bells had been silenced; only to be rung as a signal if a German invasion was underway. After three years of conflict, could there be some light at the end of the tunnel? Certainly, it seemed to most that the threat of invasion had all but gone. Even the presence of enemy aircraft overhead had diminished.

If there was any complacency, however, it was shattered for the people of Henfield when, on 30th November, a number of houses in Bramlands Lane and Lydd Hill were heavily machine gunned by low flying German aircraft - causing some damage to property but, mercifully, no casualties. The war was far from over!

34. The heat-blistered tail was all that remained of another Heinkel 111 - this time brought down at Wyckham Farm, Steyning, on 19th January, 1941, with the loss of its five crew.

35. Sgt Ben Bingley, 24, was killed when his Spitfire crashed through unexplained circumstances at Wiston on 10th March, 1941. Oxygen failure was the most likely cause.

CHICHESTER MUNICIPAL BOROUGH

Chichester, as County town of West Sussex, was the focal point for the central administration of Police, ARP and all emergency wartime services in the region and was the location of the main district Hospitals, the Royal West Sussex and St. Richards.

As evidenced by surviving records, it is clear what an important role these two hospitals played - not least of all in the treatment of casualties sustained in air attacks during the 1941 Blitz on Portsmouth and Southhampton. Many of those injured in raids on the two cities were dispersed to Chichester - partly for reasons of greater safety, partly because their local hospitals were overwhelmed with injured patients. Of course, the enormous military presence in the surrounding area gave rise to a number of Army, Navy and Royal Air Force admissions - not least of all the result of injuries sustained in flying accidents or aerial battles. Although there were no aircraft incidents within the confines of the Borough during the period of this book it will be seen from the following chapter that it was quite another story in the surrounding Chichester Rural District!

On 10th March, 1941, bombs were dropped on the city without, it appears, causing any serious damage or casualties. Perhaps the intended target was really RAF Tangmere as the raiders were back again three days later when a single enemy aircraft bombed and machine gunned the airfield from 4,000ft at quarter-to-midnight, killing one RAF serviceman.

On the night of 3rd May, 1941, two German airman parachuted down into the city and were taken prisoner by Chichester Police. They were crew members from two Heinkel 111 bombers shot down that night by Tangmere based Beaufighter of 219 Squadron, and which fell at Sidlesham and Eastergate. Residents in the city had seen and heard machine gun and cannon fire in the night sky, and watched the fiery end of the two enemy raiders.

A successful night such as this would have doubtless seen many a celebratory pint downed in the Mess at Tangmere - also in Chichester, where the local hostelry was a focal point for the social life of Tangmere's RAF personnel. "The Dolphin", "Nags Head" and "Unicorn" were all favourite watering holes. Arthur King, landlord of the "Unicorn", was especially welcoming to "his boys" from Tangmere and many a happy hour was spent away from the hurly-burly of war and privations of service life! Dances and parties were regular features, and on Wednesday, l0th December, 1941, a Grand Dance for the Aid To Russia Fund was held there - with the RAF Tangmere Dance Band and musicians of the late Ken "Snake Hips" Johnson in attendance. Johnson, a famous and popular musician of the period, had been killed earlier in the Blitz when the Cafe de Paris in London's West End was hit. The "Unicorn" was hardly the Cafe de Paris, but to its patrons it was a special place. As a pub, it no longer exists and is now a suite of offices.

Incidents of one sort or another continued in Chichester throughout l942, although there were no serious consequences. Perhaps summing up the lull in aerial activities which the City was now experiencing was an episode on 29th April, l942, when the siren sounded at Chichester Barracks at four minutes past four in the morning waking the nervous citizens from their sleep; but it was .... a false alarm! Scatterings of bombs here and there in surrounding districts caused little harm or damage in l942, and of seemingly greater hazard were unexploded AA shells which failed to detonate in the air and fell back to earth. Damage was caused at various locations on l9th June, l942, and then on 20th August the entry hole of an unexploded shell was found alongside the driveway to Oakwood House. It was subsequently dug out by the Bomb Disposal Service, but these were lethal reminders of the danger from falling military hardware which could deal death and destruction to friend and foe alike.

36. The pilots of the Tangmere Wing were pictured at Westhampnett during 1941. Seated at centre (arms folded) is the legendary legless fighter pilot, Wing Commander Douglas Bader, who led the Tangmere Wing.

➤

37. This building in St. Pancras, Chichester, was formerly the Unicorn Hotel - a favourite haunt of pilots from nearby Tangmere and Westhampnett.

38. Handbill advertising one of the regular events at Chichester's Unicorn Hotel.

AID TO RUSSIA FUND

A

Grand Dance

will be held at the

UNICORN HOTEL

on

Wednesday, Dec. 10th

Dancing 7.30 to 11.45

R.A.F. (Tangmere) Dance Band

(Members of the late Ken Johnson's Dance Band from Cafe de Paris, W. 1)

(Under the direction of John Allen)

By kind permission of the Commanding Officer

Admission 5/6 (including Refreshments)

Licence applied for

Tickets obtainable from The Unicorn

Moore & Wingham, Printers, 39 East Street. Tel. 2883

39. On 28th February, 1942, Pte. John Moore, a deserter from the Canadian Highland Light Infantry, was brought to Chichester Police Court by Det. Sgt. Heslin and P.C. Fuller, charged with the murder of Police Sgt. William Avis at Bognor on 26th February. Moore was committed for trial at the Old Bailey. (See also Bognor Regis).

When one considers the number of aircraft downed in the district for one reason or another during the years 1941 - 1942 it was, perhaps, a timely announcement from the Police which appeared in the Sussex Magazine of January, 1941. It read:-

"HUN PLANE SOUVENIRS"

"The new hobby of collecting, exchanging and selling bits and pieces of crashed Hun planes is viewed with stern official disfavour, and its fans will be well advised to moderate their enthusiasm. "Immediately a German plane is brought down" says a Sussex Police Superintendent, "there is a great rush of people to the scene, and by the time the authorities can get there, they find half the plane has been tampered with, and a great part stolen. It often happens that the parts they wish to find, and important parts, such as the instruments on the dashboard, are all gone". Prosecutions have begun, and will be continued for this "crime against the State" as it was called. It was laid down that as soon as a German plane reaches English earth it becomes the property of the Air Ministry, and anyone who pinches, scrounges or otherwise obtains parts off it is guilty of theft".

Despite this stern warning it is doubtful if it had any effect on "moderating the enthusiasm" of the schoolboy collectors who pedalled furiously to the scene of each new crash. They certainly had plenty to visit, and at least sixty aircraft came down in the Rural District between 1941 and the end of 1942. If the schoolboy collectors, however, were only looking for "Hun Machines" then they would have been largely disappointed. Of the sixty or so aircraft down, only four were German! Fortunately, schoolboys were not discerning collectors.

One of the first machines for them to visit in 1941 was Hurricane V6753 of 302 Squadron which made a forced landing at Morrels Farm, Lagness, on 2nd February. Its Polish pilot, Sgt. Markiewicz, was injured in the crash which happened after the low flying Hurricane had struck the sea. By all accounts, he must have had a lucky escape!

On the 8th of the month the almost consistently unlucky 219 Squadron lost a Beaufighter at Gumber Farm, Slindon, which crashed ten minutes after the pilot radioed that the aircraft was full of smoke. Pilot Officer Head, Sgt. Willis and Sgt. Le Dong all lost their lives. The aeroplane had come down at a dummy or decoy airfield intended to fool enemy aircraft into attacking it. Dummy aeroplanes were dispersed around the site, and at night flare paths and other lights were lit in a ruse to draw potential attackers away from nearby Tangmere. What the locals thought of the RAF's attempts to get the Germans to bomb them is

not recorded, but perhaps the feelings of Farmer Mouland of Gumber Farm are reflected in his invoice for £2.0.0 in respect of services to the RAF's contractor removing the wreckage of the Beaufighter. Apparently, he did not feel inclined to be benevolent. After all, he nightly sat at the centre of a candle flame to which the Luftwaffe were expected to be attracted!

The schoolboy collectors who arrived on the scene of the crash of a Heinkel 111 at Eastergate on 3rd May, 1941, had to scrabble amongst the rubbish of the Council Scrap Yard at Marshall's Gravel Pit for souvenirs - cars, bedsteads and bits of old iron were mixed up with the wreckage of this Heinkel whilst yet another was liberally strewn around the fields of Keynor Farm, Sidlesham, that same night. Plenty for the souvenir hunters, here!

On the night of 25th/26th June, 1941, a Junkers 88 was shot down into the sea off Selsey by a Beaufighter of 219 Squadron flown by Pilot Officer Hodgkinson and Sgt. Dye. The aeroplane exploded at around 3,000 ft and fell into the water and along the seashore near East Beach Road with the loss of all four crew. Once again, the souvenir hunters moved in but, on 28th July, 1941, the "Daily Mirror" reported a case against two local men, William Hodder and Leslie Dunnaway, who had "stolen by finding" a German radio transmitter at Selsey. Undoubtedly, this was from the Junkers 88. Both men were bound over, but it is unlikely this discouraged further souvenering !

Wing Commander Douglas Bader, the legendary legless fighter pilot, led the "Tangmere Wing" of three Spitfire fighter Squadrons during the summer of 1941, and it was on operations from Tangmere that he was brought down over France on 9th August and taken Prisoner of War. His loss was keenly felt within the Royal Air Force generally, at RAF Tangmere particularly and in the Chichester locality where he had become a familiar and well known figure.

On 7th September, 1941, two Spitfires of 129 Squadron were taking off from Westhampnett when they collided in mid-air causing the pilot of one, Sgt. Boddy, to bale out whilst the other nursed his crippled machine back to the airfield. Sgt. Boddy's Spitfire, serial number W3333, plunged to the bottom of Chichester Harbour at Birdham Lock ending the short life of a Spitfire which had been purchased through public subscription by the people of Hendon, London, and named "Hendon Pegasus". During the 1980s the wreck of the Spitfire was salvaged by enthusiasts from Tangmere Military Aviation Museum.

RAF Thorney Island was the scene of a tragic episode on 29th September, 1941, when a Hudson bomber swung off the runway, crashed and caught fire. The Station Commander, Group Captain Henry Scroggs, raced to the scene with a number of others intent on rescuing the crew when the bomb load of the Hudson exploded, killing Group Captain Scroggs and seven others. Ironically, the crew of the aeroplane had already got clear and were safe at the time of the explosion.

Throughout 1941 the rate of attrition involving aircraft of the Royal Air Force continued at an alarming pace. For example, on 5th October, 1941, two more Spitfires of 129 Squadron collided in mid air - this time with fatal results. The aircraft fell at Bowley Farm, South Mundham, and at Sefters Farm, Lagness, killing Sgt. Stuivenga (a Rhodesian) and a Sgt. Smith. An unusual loss was a Fairy Seal bi-plane of the Fleet Air Arm, based at Ford, and down at Balsams Farm, Funtington, on 21st October but with its three crew safe. 219 Squadron had also been in a rough time again, having the squadron's "hack" Magister down at Barnham Court on 10th October and a Beaufighter lost with both crew at Peckhams Copse, Merston, on 28th October and then a further two crew members killed when their Beaufighter flew into the ground at Croucham Hill, Fontwell, on 28th October. The damage being inflicted on the Luftwaffe by 219 Squadron across the night skies of Southern England was considerable and yet it was being conducted against a background of losses through accidents which must have been hard for any squadron to sustain.

1942 opened in much the same way, with an accident claiming a Havoc aircraft of 1455 Flight at Oughton when an air lock in the fuel system resulted in a wheels-up emergency landing. The aeroplane was viewed with much curiosity by the locals, having a huge searchlight mounted in the nose part of the fuselage. 1455 Flt had been formed as a "Turbinlite Unit" - in reality, flying searchlights to illuminate German bombers for the night fighters to deal with. It was, literally, a crashing failure - as will be seen later!

Yet again, 219 Squadron was suffering.

This time, on the 5th June, a pilot was unable to lower his landing gear returning from a night flight and was instructed by Tangmere to "fly around until dawn". Sadly, the aeroplane later crashed at Halnaker Park, Boxgrove, killing Sgt's Smee and Bassett. Later that summer, on 4th August, yet another of the fated 1455 Flt. Turbinlite Havocs crashed - this time spinning into the ground at Oving with fatal results.

Mystery surrounds the loss of a 169 Squadron Mustang which crashed vertically into the ground at Marden on 15th August, killing Flying Officer G.B. Penman who was engaged on a cross-country flight. The reason for the crash is obscure, but even stranger is the case of Penman himself. Records show his body was returned to the family at Waverley, Edinburgh, but by some strange quirk no burial place for him has ever been located! Even the War Graves Commission are perplexed and having no knowledge of his burial place have concluded he has no known grave. This is just one of those many mysteries thrown up by the strange events of war.

With the Dieppe Raid in full swing on 19th August, 1942, a Junkers 88 crashed through trees on the brow of a hill at Colworth Farm, Westdean, and exploded with the loss of all four crew. Even today, tiny shreds of aluminium are to be found strewn in amongst the narrow strip of trees through which the aeroplane crashed.

24th October saw the first Lancaster aircraft down in Sussex when a crippled 49 Squadron aeroplane was apparently attempting to land at Ford and struck a barn at Wicks Farm, crashed, and caught fire twenty yards from the farm house. Five of the crew are buried together at Littlehampton cemetery and include a holder of the DFC and two DFM recipients. Another crew member died later that day in hospital at Chichester from burns.

Losses through accident continued almost unabated and with regular monotony until the end of the year - the last being recorded on the 29th December when a Hurricane of 534 Squadron crashed on the perimeter of Tangmere aerodrome.

Throughout all this mayhem the Luftwaffe had been noticeably absent from the skies over Sussex - only comparatively few raids being made during the period. However, with the RAF destroying its own aircraft at such an alarming rate there was hardly any need for the German airforce to intervene! Nevertheless, as a timely reminder that they were still there and able to hit almost when and where they chose, two bombs were released from low level over Selsey on the 3rd September, 1942, at 11.00 am - the third anniversary, to the minute, of the declaration of war. Both bombs ricocheted, one passing through the chimney of the Marine Hotel before exploding in mid air over Clayton Road and the other smashing through a garage before detonating in the air over Peachey Road causing extensive damage. The Clayton Road bomb caused serious injury to about thirty U.S. Navy personnel and four civilians. The Luftwaffe had been infrequent visitors to these parts lately, but they could still hit hard! All told it had been a hectic, tragic, fraught and noisy period for this Rural District area. As we shall see in our next volume, it got worse before it got better!

41. The receipted invoice to A.V. Nicholls of Brighton for services rendered in assisting in removal of a crashed Beaufighter at Gumber Farm, Slindon, during February, 1941.

40. The stalwart Home Guard of Pagham march past a bombed out bunglaow, led by their C.O., Captain Curry.

42. German airmen who were killed over Britain were buried with full military honours by the RAF. Here, the funeral cortege for the crew of the Junkers 88 which crashed at RAF Thorney Island on 18th April, 1941, passes the Officers Mess. Note the swastika draped coffins.

43. This was all that remained after a Junkers 88 had smashed through trees at Colworth Farm, Westdean, on 19th August, 1942, extinguishing the lives of four young airmen as it exploded.

44. Another view of the scattered debris from the Junkers 88 down at Colworth Farm.

45. This granite memorial was erected in 1942 in Clymping Churchyard by men of Ford Air Station to the memory of those who had died in the attack of 18th August, 1940. The barbed wire perimeter of the aerodrome can be seen, with the camouflaged hangars beyond.

47. Spitfire W3333 "Hendon Pegasus" was one of four fighter aircraft purchased by the citizens of Hendon. This was one of the savings stamp cards issued to fund contributors. On 7th September, 1941, the fruit of these contributions went to the bottom of Chichester Harbour!

46. Spitfire W3333, "Hendon Pegasus", ended up in Chichester Harbour at Birdham Lock on 7th September, 1941, after a mid air collision with another Spitfire. Sgt. Boddy baled out safely.

48. Crumpled wreckage of the Heinkel lll mixed up with the contents of the Corporation Scrapyard at Eastergate where the bomber crashed on 3rd May, 1941.

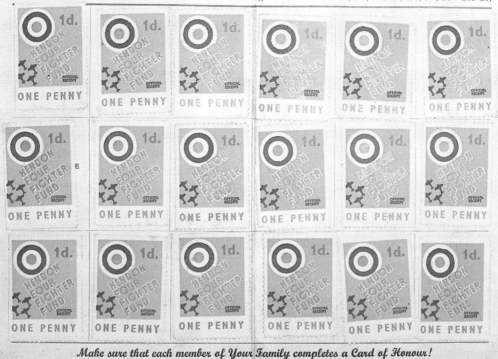

BOROUGH OF HENDON FOUR FIGHTER FUND. Under the patronage of His Worship the Mayor of Hendon (Councillor A. A. Naar, M.B.E., J.P.) and Sir Reginald Blair, M.P. *Chairman of Organising Committee :* Councillor Kirkland Bridge.

Fighter Fund Poster Stamps are obtainable in the following denominations : 1d., 3d., 6d., 1/-, 2/6, 5/-, 10/- and £1.

Make sure that each member of Your Family completes a Card of Honour!

49. RAF Station, Thorney Island, photographed on 7th November, 1941. Careful inspection reveals parked aeroplanes and another taking off from the camouflaged runway. On 29th September, 1941, a Hudson crashed on take-off and blew up killing the Station Commander and seven others. Note the bombed out shell of the top left hand hangar - hit by Stuka dive bombers on 18th August, 1940.

50. RAF Westhampnett (now Goodwood Airfield) was a satellite field to RAF Tangmere, its "parent" station. Westhampnett housed a variety of fighter squadrons from 1940 onwards. Here a Spitfire of 616 Squadron undergoes open air maintenance.

CUCKFIELD RURAL DISTRICT

In common with inland districts, this particular area suffered little during the 1941-1942 period in respect of bombing incidents, air raid damage or casualties - much of this being reserved for the seaside areas which took the brunt of "Hit and Run" raiders.

On the night of 1st/2nd June, 1941, there was excitement in the Devils Dyke and Poynings area when a Junkers 88 was shot down at Wickhurst Barns minutes after midnight. The victor was a Wing Commander Allen, of our often mentioned 219 Squadron based at Tangmere. (Perhaps this book should have been sub-titled "219 Squadron's Fortunes of War!"). The stricken German bomber crashed in flames and disintegrated after three of the crew had baled out. Two, Feldwebel Stein and Feldwebel Riedel, were captured almost immediately and another, Gefreiter Rosenhahn, failed to escape and was killed in the crash. A huge search was mounted for the fourth man, but it was not until morning that the body of Feldwebel Karl Illsemann was found on the South Downs, his parachute having failed to open.

The crashed Junkers 88 attracted it's usual horde of sightseers and souvenir hunters - in this case causing the Police some embarrassment when two machine guns were taken by trophy hunters despite a Police presence. Five youths were seen cycling from the scene, one with a heavy sack and another with a machine gun strapped to his back. If they avoided eventual Police discovery, one wonders where those souvenirs are today!

Another night-time episode involved a Defiant of 264 Squadron which crashed at Slaugham Park when Flying Officer W.Knocker baled out with his gunner on 31st August, 1941, after losing control of his aircraft. Defiant N 3453 dived into trees and exploded, but this was not the first time Knocker had abandoned a Defiant over Sussex! (See also Uckfield Rural District). On the same date, 31st August, another aircraft crashed not far from the Junkers 88 at Poynings when Sgt. W. Kenwood of 92 Squadron baled out of Spitfire W 3120.

As previously stated, there was little in the way of bombing incidents of note during the 1941-1942 period which affected the Cuckfield area, although reports indicate some damage being caused in the vicinity by bombs on the night of 8th/9th March 1941.

1942 was similarly uneventful, and possibly the most memorable and notable event happened at Pilstye Farm, Cuckfield, on 17th June when a Spitfire of 602 Squadron crashed killing a Norwegian pilot, Sgt. Ole Aarebrot, who is thought to have suffered oxygen failure at 23,000 ft. His was another tragic loss through accident, and yet another case of oxygen failure. The crash, however, is vivid in the memory of those who witnessed or heard the tortured scream of the over-revving Rolls Royce Merlin before being silenced in a thudding explosion as the Spitfire disintegrated in the corner of a wheat field. The impact with the sandstone soil strata literally caused the aeroplane to totally fragment, leaving little of any consequence for the salvage gang to clear. Sgt. Aarebrot had endured enormous difficulty in getting to England to continue the fight against Germany and his death in this manner was a tragic waste of one who colleagues called "one of Norway's finest". A fellow Norwegian, completing Ole's last Log Book entry, marked the sign of a cross and R.I.P.

And, with apologies to Rupert Brooke, wrote "There is some corner of a Sussex field that is forever Norway".

51. Sgt. Ole Aarebrot, a Norwegian, was pilot of a Spitfire which crashed at Pilstye Farm, Cuckfield. He became yet another victim of a tragic flying accident probably caused by oxygen failure.

CUCKFIELD URBAN
DISTRICT

Noteworthy was the part played in the war effort by the Hurstwood Park War Emergency Hospital, Haywards Heath, which provided specialist treatment for air raid victims from across a wide catchment area of Sussex, Kent, Surrey, Hampshire and London. In addition, specialist paediatric care was provided for infant air raid victims at Elfinswood Auxiliary Hospital, Haywards Heath. It is impossible to say how many severely injured civilians were nursed back to health here although, inevitably, there were those who did not pull through despite the excellent standard of care. These fatalities are listed on the Civilian War Dead Register for the Urban District, thus giving a falsely inflated figure of civilian war casualties in the area. In reality, the casualties at Hurstwood Park had been injured in incidents as far apart as Dover, Peckham Rye, and Bletchingley but, in common with neighbouring Burgess Hill, the district had minimal air raid activity in 1941 and 1942 and experienced no civilian fatalities of its own.

In an incident on 19th February, 1942, a Photo Reconnaissance Spitfire PR IV of No. 1 Photo Reconnaissance Unit crashed in attempting a forced landing at Shepherds Hill, Haywards Heath. The report states that Pilot Officer F. E. Nettleton was injured when landing in ".....difficult country". His Spitfire, however, was repaired and lived to fight another day!

If Nettleton's landing had been in "difficult country" then the survival of the seven crew of a Halifax bomber at nearby Great Bentley Farm, had been nothing short of a miracle, given that the four engined bomber landed in similar country - and at night! The bomber, from 158 Squadron, landed at 02.30 hours after an operational flight and hit trees, haystack and a shed before catching fire. Four of the crew were slightly hurt, but the captain, Pilot Officer Beveridge, was later severely criticised for this his second similar accident inside a month. The cause of the Cuckfield accident was stated to be due to a combination of heavy petrol consumption and pilot error, and records show that the unfortunate Beveridge never flew with 158 Squadron again. Perhaps, though, one should first consider the flying skills of Beveridge in getting this huge bomber and its crew down relatively intact in pitch darkness - albeit that error had led to the mishaps in the first instance. Very often, those like Beveridge were inexperienced young men of twenty or so who were being tested to the very limits of physical and mental endurance. Unfortunately, an Air Force Board of Inquiry was unlikely to take such factors into account.

52. Sgt. A.E.F. Wheeler, 158 Squadron, was the Flight Engineer of the Halifax which crashed at Great Bentley Farm, Cuckfield, on 16th November, 1942. He was one the seven crew lucky to survive this incident and is pictured here later in the war after being commissioned.

COUNTY BOROUGH OF EASTBOURNE

Eastbourne earned itself the dubious reputation of being the most raided town in the South East, and the years 1941 and 1942 were to see some harrowing events. However, the period opened with relative inactivity which was broken on the 24th February when a Polish pilot, Sgt. Rogowski of 74 Squadron, was forced to make a crash landing in Spitfire P7559 at Langney Green. Although injured, it is reported that his main concern seemed to be about his wrist watch which had broken in the crash!

Then, in March, the bombers returned. On the 12th a scattering of bombs across the town caused relatively little in the way of casualties or damage. The raid on the 28th, however, was more serious. Bombs dropped from a low flying Dornier 17 hit the Roselands area causing considerable damage and the loss of three lives with twenty five injured.

Again, there were raids on May 9th, 11th and 24th and another on June 7th. Damage and casualties were sustained, but 1942 would prove to be worse by far.

It was on 4th May, 1942, that the "Hit and Run" raids began for Eastbourne when nine Messesschmitt 109's streaked across the town from Beachy Head, firing machine guns and cannon as they each released a single bomb on the town. Damage was widespread and severe; Willingdon Road, Commercial Road, Winchcombe Road, Finmere Road, the Cavendish Hotel, Railway Station, Locomotive Sheds and the Gasworks were all hit. At the Cavendish Hotel, in use by the RAF's No.1 Air Navigation School, the eastern wing was demolished killing a WAAF, an airman and two civilians. Three others were killed, and thirty six injured - offshore, the fleeing raiders shot up a fishing boat, injuring Alec Huggett and Alex "Micky" Andrews in an episode repeated off Icklesham on 16th September (see Battle Rural District). Three days later, on 7th May, four more fighter bombers delivered their deadly loads to the town, killing one, injuring thirty one and, once more, causing widespread damage through bomb damage and gunfire.

May 20th saw two Messerschmitt 109's attacking shipping south-west of Newhaven. Attacking a Corvette at low-level Unteroffizier Oswald Fischer saw his bomb bounce off the sea and over his target just as his aircraft was hit by machine gun fire from his intended victim. With a faltering engine Fischer was forced to land at Half Way House between Beachy Head and East Dean - thus presenting the RAF with an almost intact machine! Repaired, the aeroplane was later test flown for evaluation purposes by the RAF.

These sharp daylight attacks, however, almost paled into insignificance on 11th August, when a large night raid used flares to illuminate the town before forty seven high explosive and two thousand incendiary bombs rained down. Damage was widespread, but casualties were remarkably light when considering the number of bombs dropped. All the same, three civilians were killed as were eight Canadian soldiers who's unit had just arrived in the town. Given the scale of the attack, and the impending Dieppe raid which would involve Canadian troops it was inevitable that questions would be asked about security. Suddenly, the impact of the "Careless Talk Costs Lives" slogan hit home for the townsfolk of Eastbourne. Had there been a breach of security?

The momentum of the fighter bomber raids continued on 13th August when four Focke Wulf 190's crossed the coast at Cooden and headed west. Two bombs dropped at Pevensey Bay and the two delivering aircraft peeled off for home, leaving the other pair to head for Eastbourne dropping their bombs at Roseveare Road and on the Gasworks where one gasholder was hit and set on fire. The town was also raked with gunfire in what was, now, a typical "Hit and Run" raid.

On the 26th August the most memorable raid of its type took place on the town - memorable because it resulted in the destruction of one of the two raiding Focke- Wulf 190's. As the aircraft roared in over Pevensey Bay they opened fire with cannon and machine gun, hitting fisherman Alfred Grant as he worked on the beach. Being a fisherman was clearly an unhealthy occupation when the fighter bombers were about!

Coming over the Crumbles the two aircraft released their bombs on Marlow Avenue and the Electricity Works, killing three and injuring seven. However, as they passed Caffyns Garage a Bren-gun manned by Canadians on the garage roof had opened up on them and, moments later, one of the aircraft crashed inverted into a ditch alongside Lottbridge Drove. Its pilot, Oberfeldwebel Werner Kassa, was decapitated in the crash which may or may not have been the result of gunfire. Other theories have been advanced, suggesting instead the aeroplane was caught in the blast of the bombs or else simply crashed trying to avoid defensive fire. Whatever, its destruction was a welcome morale-booster for the townsfolk.

October 26th saw another heavy loss of life when a Dornier 217 released its deadly cargo of four 250Kg bombs on the Seaside area, hitting Willoughby Crescent, the Southbourne Road area and destroying the Alexandra Arms pub. In total, fifteen died and twenty two people were injured.

Despite wartime austerity, Christmas saw the shoppers out in numbers on December 18th when another Dornier 217 released four bombs on the town centre, hitting shops at 45 to 53 Terminus Road. Amongst those shops destroyed was Marks & Spencer's and a desperate 48 hour attempt got under way to release trapped victims. In total, eighteen died and thirty seven were injured with a further nine injured from falling debris during rescue work. It was an appalling pre-Christmas tragedy, but the fighter bombers were back again on the 29th when two Focke Wulf 190's ripped across the town accompanied by the now familiar rattle of gun fire and crump of exploding bombs - this time it was the turn of Victoria Drive and Moat Croft Road to bear the brunt of an attack which left two dead and another thirty six injured. It had been a miserable and unforgettable time for the town which was yet to suffer another two years of frequent air attack.

53. This was the swathe of damage cut through Churchdale Road and Willoughby Crescent, Eastbourne, during the air raid on 28th March, 1941.

54. A particularly nasty raid was that suffered by Eastbourne on 4th May, 1942, when nine Messerschmitt 109's bombed the town. Seven people were killed and thirty six injured. The Railway Station, shown here, was among the several targets badly hit.

55. The effects of blast on a house in St. Anne's Road, Eastbourne, after a raid on 11th August, 1942.

56. On 20th May, 1942, Unteroffizier Oswald Fischer landed his Messerschmitt 109-F at Halfway House, between Beachy Head and East Dean. This aeroplane was later repaired and test flown by the RAF. Note the painted white bomb on rear fuselage.

57. Caffyn's Garage, in common with most other commercial enterprises, was turned across largely to war work. The Seaside, Eastbourne, works became an Army vehicle repair depot. Here, women mechanics work on a Quad Gun Tractor.

58. Oberfeldwebel Werner Kassa died when his Focke Wulf 190 crashed into a ditch at Lottbridge Drove, Eastbourne, during an attack on 26th August, 1942. It was claimed as shot down by Canadian Bren-Gunners on the roof of Caffyns Garage nearby.

EAST GRINSTEAD URBAN DISTRICT

The Queen Victoria Cottage Hospital in the town is famous for its burns unit which, by 1941, had achieved notable acclaim for work in re-' building the faces and lives of pilots badly burned during the Battle of Britain. Ward Three, under the pioneering guidance of the renowned plastic surgeon Sir Archibald McIndoe, went on to treat hundreds of badly burned allied airmen thoughout the war and the convalescing fliers were a familiar sight around the town.

East Grinstead was spared any heavy air attacks and had no civilian loss of life during the 1941 to 1942 period. However, early in 1941 a 500kg bomb fell near Hoskyns Farm, Holtye Road, but failed to explode. For several days nearby residents were evacuated and local traffic diverted whilst a bomb disposal unit dealt with the device which, defused, was eventually displayed in the Urban Council Offices at Norton House.

On 5th June of that year a Lysander aircraft of 239 Squadron from Gatwick got lost in fog and tried to land at Hill Place Farm. In doing so it ran into trees and crashed. The aeroplane was wrecked, but Pilot Officer Bonniface and Sgt. Watson were lucky to escape with their lives.

Another Gatwick based aeroplane, this time a Tiger Moth, developed engine trouble and, in the gathering darkness, landed undamaged at Hackenden Field, Holtye Road, on the 10th February, 1942. Pilot Officer Marshall and Flt. Sgt. Healy were uninjured in the episode.

Later in 1942, on 26th October, the town had a miraculous escape when a stick of bombs were dropped across the town hitting West Hill, Brooklands, Queens Road Cemetery, a swimming pool and falling across fields, gardens and open spaces. There was widespread damage and destruction, but not a single casualty was sustained. The following week a thanksgiving service was held in the Parish Church which was packed to capacity. Those present could not know that less than a year later it would be a rather different picture when the same congregation packed the same church for a memorial service to those killed in the county's worst air raid disaster.

59. When an unexploded bomb fell near Hoskyns Farm, East Grinstead in 1941 it took several days of work before it could be rendered safe by men of the Royal Engineers Bomb Disposal Unit. No amount of praise would be sufficient for the bomb disposal men who carried out thousands of similar unpleasant and highly dangerous disposal operations.

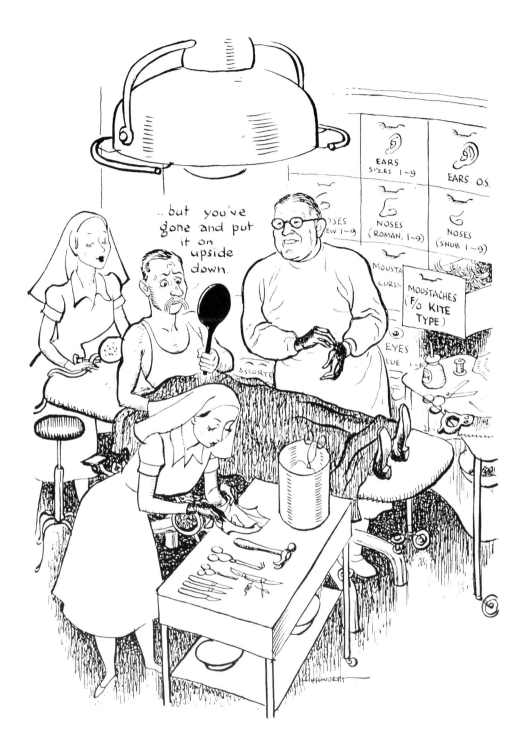

60. The black humour of the "Guinea Pigs". Badly burned airmen of the RAF commissioned this cartoon by Illingworth depicting the great surgeon, Sir Archibald McIndoe, at work in East Grinstead's Royal Victoria Hospital.

Although the threat of invasion had, in effect, receded after 1940 the preparations for defending Britain against occupation continued well into 1941 and 1942. Indeed, the market town of Hailsham was declared a "Nodal Point" in 1941 along with other strategically important towns and villages in the South East. This classification meant that the town was: *"A defended locality, situated usually at strategically important road junctions, garrisoned normally by local Home Guards, with the addition of any available troops stationed in the vicinity, and intended to restrict, delay or hamper the operation of enemy invaders until reserves and reinforcements could be brought up"*

In reality, this meant the town was closely ringed with "Dragons' Teeth" concrete tank traps, barbed wire, road blocks and anti-tank mines whilst defensive firing positions were set up in all the principal town centre buildings. To what extent the civilian population realised their town was to be defended at all costs in an almost "do-or-die" scenario is debatable. What is certain, however, is that the population had been under no illusions at all about the prospect of invasion during the first part of the war - and the highly visible defensive preparations brought home the message of impending danger! So, too, did the innumerable road blocks in the district. Manned by Police and armed soldiers, all vehicles, including lorries, buses and bicycles were stopped and civilians questioned as to destination and their Identity Cards examined. Even a relatively short bus journey from Heathfield to Hailsham could result in passengers being stopped anything up to six or seven times and asked to produce identification! Persons not authorised to be in what was a restricted area could be turned away. Today, it is hard to imagine this "front line" aspect of the war which was brought to the region's leafy lanes, although careful observers can still note the occasional pill-box strong point or old tank traps scattered around the countryside and now subject to preservation orders. In the Nodal Point of Hailsham, however, little trace remains today of its intended function in the event of invasion.

In common with the rest of the United Kingdom, there was a marked decrease in German air activity from the mid-summer of 1941 through to the end of 1942. Primarily, this was a consequence of German attention being turned on Russia and throughout 1941 there was not a single German aircraft downed in the Hailsham Rural District area, and no civilian casualties through air attack during the years 1941 to 1942. In fact, only one German aircraft fell in the district during 1942, although no less than sixteen RAF aircraft came to grief during the two year period.

The first of these was a Spitfire which crashed on the 5th March, 1941, just to the north of the disused pre-war civilian aerodrome at Wilmington. Its pilot, Sgt. Hamer of No. 61 Operational Training Unit, was trapped in the wreckage and died before he could be rescued.

On the 18th of that month a formation of six Hurricanes from 17 Squadron based at Croydon were flying over the district en-route to Ford and Shoreham when they sighted five aircraft in the direction of Bexhill which they took to be Spitfires. Moments later the five "Spitfires" were roaring in to attack the Hurricanes, despatching two within seconds of each other. Sgt. Pilots Hughes and Bartlett were forced to bale out, not even having seen what had hit them. In fact, the "Spitfires" were Messerschmitt 109's which rapidly departed southwards with no hint of interference from the remaining Hurricanes. So quick was the engagement and so complete the surprise that none of the British pilots realised what was happening until it was all over. Sgt. Hughes drifted down on his parachute as his Hurricane dived vertically into a meadow at Stream Farm, Chiddingly, burying itself deeply on impact with the soil. Bartlett also baled out, and his Hurricane crashed at Blackboys (see Uckfield Rural District.)

The following day, Sgt. Pilot Eade of 610 Squadron also fell victim to Messerschmitt l09's, being " bounced " off Calais and making it as far as Thorneyfold Farm, Bodle Street, before crash landing his Spitfire with shrapnel wounds in his arm and shoulder.

A few miles away at Oak Glen Farm, Horam, two 250 Kg bombs fell on 23rd March caused no damage. Nevertheless, they were reminders that the Luftwaffe was likely to strike anywhere, anytime.

To the south of the district, at Friston, the RAF had established a forward satellite airfield on the Downs between Gayles Farm and the Seven Sisters Cliffs during May 1941. It was later to become a busy and important aerodrome for RAF Fighter Command. In the early days of its wartime use, however, there were no resident squadrons but on 7th July 616 Squadron flew in from Tangmere to use the aerodrome as a forward operating base for their Spitfires. Landing into a rising dawn sun, Sgt "Jeff" West made a bad landing on the unfamiliar field and ended up crashing - breaking off undercarriage legs and propeller blades. West was unhurt and cleared of any blame for what was probably the first of many RAF and USAAF air crashes on the field. "Jeff" West would later be involved in a more spectacular episode in September of 1941 (See Bexhill Municipal Borough).

Two days later Sgt. Pilot Warne crashed his Spitfire at Herstmonceux Castle, and there was then a lull in the occurrence of any aircraft related incidents until 18th October when a Miles Magister of 402 Squadron, RCAF, came down at New Barn Gate, West Dean.

Although the "Hit and Run" raids of 1942 were primarily against coastal towns, there was an unusual episode on 28th April when two Messerchmitt 109's carried out a low level attack on the Horam area at 8.15 pm, dropping 250 Kg bombs at Chestnuts Farm and Lotus Lands. There was little damage, and no casualties reported. What the intended target could have been in this rural area is unclear. There were no buildings or military installations of any note, and only the Railway Station possibly being a worthwhile aiming point.

On the 5th May, Pilot Officer Edward Hall, an Australian serving with 129 Squadron at Westhampnett, abandoned his burning Spitfire high above Wilmington after being hit by anti-aircraft fire over France. He landed safely, and left his Spitfire to crash at Endlewick Farm, Arlington.

Throughout the remainder of the year there followed a miscellany of Spitfires and Hurricanes crashing or crash-landing around the district but, on 7th December, a Focke Wulf 190 flew into Oxendean Hill, Jevington, in poor visibility, killing 22 year old Willi Muskatewitz as his aeroplane exploded on impact. Almost certainly he was commencing a run-in to attack Eastbourne - a favourite tactic being to cross the coast at Birling Gap and then arc round on their target from the North-West, bombing

and machine gunning the town on the way out to sea. As the wreckage and mutilated body of Muskatewitz was cleared away the district could look forward to more than another two years of warfare. The days of the Battle of Britain in 1940 had, undoubtedly, been the most hectic and eventful yet. However, there were dark and dangerous times ahead.

61. On 7th July, 1941, Sgt. Jeff West of 616 Squadron suffered this landing mishap in Spitfire P7829,YQ-B, at Friston aerodrome. White sheets have been laid out across wings and fuselage to mark the stranded fighter as a hazard to other aircraft landing or taking-off.

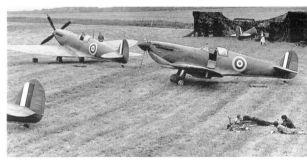

62. In June, 1988, Spitfires again returned to Friston for filming of the TV drama series "Piece of Cake". These are actually full-sized replicas, but real Spitfires used the field as well during 1988 for the first time since 1944!

63. The Hailsham built Hurricane. Over 500 of these rather crude dummy Hurricanes were constructed at Green Brothers factory, Western Road, Hailsham. Made from wood and canvas they were placed on decoy airfields and, from the air, were convincing enough replicas.

64. These young lads, pictured in Gordon Road, Hailsham, helped the war effort by fund raising for the Red Cross. For a few coppers the Union Flag would be raised to reveal the boys' home made models of tanks and aeroplanes. On the extreme left of the picture can just be seen one of the "Dragons Teeth" tank traps which ringed Hailsham.

65. Bringing up the buried Rolls Royce Merlin engine in 1974 from the Hurricane shot down at Stream Farm, Chiddingly, on 18th March, 1941.

66. Officers of 20th (Sussex) Battalion, Home Guard, at an exercise on the South Downs during 1942. Had invasion come, these men would have led the defence of Hailsham.

67. "Halt! Identity Cards, please!" All vehicles were subject to being stopped for a check on occupants. Here, a Southdown bus comes under scrutiny by armed soldiers at a road block. This was a familiar scenario around the Nodal Point of Hailsham.

HASTINGS COUNTY BOROUGH

Hastings seaside location resulted in a number of casualties being washed up onto its beaches during the war, and 1941 was no exception. Mostly the casualties were airmen. On 31st January the body of a German flier was washed ashore at Glyne Gap and, on the same day, another was found at the Bathing Pool, St.Leonards.

On the 7th of the next month the sea delivered up another of its dead when an Able Seaman from the *SS Stanwold* was found on the foreshore at Eversfield Place. How he came to be there is a mystery, because the *Stanwold* was sunk ten miles WSW of Selsey Bill on the 27th of that month.

On the same day that the German airmen had been found at Glyne Gap and St. Leonards the Luftwaffe was overhead again, releasing five bombs - two of which failed to explode. Clyde Road, Gensing Gardens and Woodland Vale were all hit in this attack but it was at the height of the Blitz, on 8th April, that a particularly heavy attack was experienced. Two aeroplanes dropped twenty eight high explosive bombs and 300 incendiaries across the town hitting the Railway Station, Stanley Road, Priory Avenue, St. Helens Crescent and Cornwallis Gardens. The Royal East Sussex Hospital and Municipal Hospital were also hit. At the former, Nurse Dorothy Gardner threw herself across patients to protect them from a falling bomb. In doing so she was seriously injured and was later awarded the George Medal in recognition of her heroism.

In common with other coastal towns, Hastings took its share of the fast, low flying fighter-bomber attacks which were very much a feature of 1942. On 5th January, 1942, a raiding force of Messerschmitt 109's shot up the sea front with cannon and machine gun fire but were given a warm reception from the local anti-aircraft guns. A reminder of this raid may still be seen in a neat bullet hole "tearing" the skirts of Queen Victoria's bronze statue at Warrior Square. A tragic consequence of an-other such raid on 3rd May was the death of little Deirdre Battersby, the two year old daughter of the Revd. and Mrs. Battersby of Emmanuel Church. The vicarage was hit by one of the bombs dropped from four Messerchmitt 109's which attacked the town shortly after 9pm. The Vicar was away, but Mrs. Battersby, herself injured, stood by the rubble as rescuers toiled to find the child. At 2 am the next morning her tiny body was found in her cot, one of the younger victims of the air war over the county.

On 2nd June two Spitfires collided over the Broomgrove area, falling in gardens at 141 Parker Road, and Ravine Lodge, Hoadswood Road. Sgt. Victor Reed and Sgt. Robert Guillerman, both of 81 Squadron, lost their lives in this tragic accident. The records show that Reed had a waterproof bag containing French bank notes - his escape currency in the event of being brought down over France. The reports go on to state that Guillerman's flying gloves and boots were marked "Willie". These rather sad little personal details are added to by the official Air Ministry report of the accident which simply puts this episode down to "one of the misfortunes of war."

The "Hit and Run" raids continued in August with bombs on Boyne Road and Berlin Road on 22nd, and again on 21st September when bombs hit the top floors of Marine Court. A more serious raid took place on 24th of that month, when seven Focke Wulf 190's, and an escort of other fighters, hit the town. Warrior Square was particularly badly hit in this attack which left 23 dead and 43 injured.

The 190's were back again on 17th October, this time hitting St. Columba's Church, Warrior Gardens and Pevensey Road. Two people died in this attack and 16 were injured.

The year ended with machine gun attacks on 7th and 21st December; one person being killed by gunfire on the 21st. Not by a long way had the town seen the last of these frightening and deadly attacks.

68. In the tragic bombing incident on 3rd May, 1942, Emmanuel Church, Hastings, was hit. The daughter of the Vicar, two year old Deirdre Battersby, was killed as she slept in her cot at the Vicarage next door.

69. Nearby, Emmanuel Road was devastated by bomb blast and an elderly couple, James and Mary Gamblen, were killed.

70. Fighter-bombers took this gap out of properties in Warrior Square, St. Leonards-on-Sea, on 24th September, 1942. Seven raiders dropped bombs which left 23 dead and 43 injured.

71. This was West Ascent after the Focke Wulf 190's had come visiting on 17th October, 1942. Two people died in this attack and sixteen were injured.

HORSHAM RURAL DISTRICT

No 49 Maintenance Unit, RAF Faygate, continued to collect vast quantities of wrecked aeroplanes - allied and enemy - from its catchment area across Southern England and, on 13th February, 1941, they did not have far to go for a Beaufighter which had crashed at Needs Farm, Partridge Green.

The two crew had abandoned the aeroplane at night after it suffered severe vibration problems. Yet again, the aircraft involved was from 219 Squadron, Tangmere, whose machinery was adding considerably to 49 M.U's collection of wreckage!.

One month later, however, on 13th March, it was a victim of 219 Squadron which the boys of Faygate's M.U. were sent to collect. This time it was a Heinkel lll which had crashed at night on Smokehouse Farm, Shipley, having fallen to the guns of Sgts. Clandillion and Dodgie. All four crew members died as the wreckage spread itself over and on Smokehouse Farm. The four were later buried with full military honours at Horsham (Hills Road) Cemetery.

Just over a month was to pass before another raider would fall in the district - this time a Junkers 88 which crashed at Slinfold. It was the night of 19th April when those in the locality heard the awful sound of over-revving aero engines in a screaming terminal dive. The noise seemed to go on for several minutes, before ending in an explosion and fireball as the bomber plunged into a small copse at the appropriately named Slaughter Bridge. The four crew were blown to pieces, and there are grisly local tales of the terrible aftermath at the scene witnessed the following morning. The aeroplane had been on its way back from bombing London when hit by Anti-Aircraft gunfire.

Yet another Junkers 88 came to grief in the District on the night on 27/28th July when it was shot down to crash at Bines Road, Partridge Green. All four crewman perished as the bomber fell to the guns of a nightfighter Beaufighter - once again, the notable 219 Squadron! The doomed bomber smashed itself across several houses and cottages before gouging out a long fire blackened furrow in an adjacent meadow. Miraculously, there were no casualties in the village although several people were rendered temporarily homeless.

The following morning the victorious Beaufighter crew, Pilot Officer Hodgkinson and Sgt. Dye, visited the scene of devastation from Tangmere and met some of the villagers affected. This was a much appreciated gesture, and they left with the villagers warm best wishes after offering their own words of comfort to those whose homes had been wrecked. Today, a large black rubber "skid" mark survives on the end wall of one of the houses, marking where one of the Junkers 88's landing wheels had hit.

It is of interest to note that in the Roman Catholic Churchyard at West Grinstead maybe found the war grave of Captain Peter Belloc, son of the famous writer Hilaire Belloc. Captain Belloc was Hilaire's youngest son and died at the age of 36 on 2nd April, 1941, but was not strictly speaking a casualty of the war and died from pneumonia. The eldest son of the family, Louis, had been killed as a pilot in the Royal Flying Corps during 1918.

With much of the Luftwaffe activity over the British Isles now confined to night time operation it was considered vital to maintain a good "black out" and there were heavy penalties for offenders. Of course, it would be reasonable to assume that members of Air Raid Precautions, Civil Defence etc. would appreciate the need for a properly maintained black out - "Put that light out" being a catch-phrase now associated very much with the Blitz period. It is, therefore, surprising to note that the West Sussex County Times recorded on 19th December, 1941, that a local Fire Watcher was among the black-out offenders fined in Horsham Magistrates Court!

January 1942 saw Henry Hall's Guest Night broadcasting live from the Odeon, Horsham , and it was no doubt a thrill for the local population to listen to the BBC programme on their wireless sets.

A departure from the rather more glamorous "Spitfire Fund" (see Horsham Urban District) was fund-raising in the locality for the purchase of Horsham's own submarine and, in February 1942, it was noted that sufficient funds had almost been raised for HMS Una, Horsham's adopted ship. This great outpouring of patriotic generosity did not pass the Army by, either! In August, 1942, "Tanks For Attack Week" was launched and two tanks were purchased and named after Horsham. In little over a year the people of the Horsham area had contributed one Spitfire, one submarine and two tanks to the overall war effort. This was not an uncommon effort on the part played by local communities in backing the war with hard cash. Indeed, it typifies the spirit of the times.

On 2nd October, 1942, a Spitfire ran out of fuel and made a forced landing at Sights Farm, Partridge Green, leaving the aeroplane slightly damaged and Sgt. Pilot H.R. Kelly of 501 Sqn. unhurt. This particular Spitfire could be repaired and flown again, and indeed was back in service by the following August. It is interesting to speculate that, had the Spitfire been wrecked, the people of Horsham could probably have raised sufficient funds for another brand new Spitfire had they been called upon to do so. Already the area had shown itself willing and able to raise funds not only for a submarine and for tanks, but also for its "own" Spitfire.

72. Wreckage was strewn far and wide when a Heinkel lll was shot down at Smokehouse Farm, Shipley, on 13th March, 1941.

73. Another piece landed on the roof of the farmhouse.

74. The four crew died in the crash and had no use for the parachutes scattered with the wreckage.

75. Inside an outhouse one of the bomber's propellers came to rest. The incident had almost devastated the farm.

76. The men of 49 Maintenance Unit return to their Faygate base with a Polish Spitfire, damaged in a crash landing in Sussex.

77. A parachute release box and harness buckles from the Junkers 88 shot down at Slaughter Bridge, Slinfold, on 19th April, 1941, tell their own grim story. All four crew members were killed in the crash.

78. Bines Road, Partridge Green, was the scene of demise for another Junkers 88 on the night of 27th/28th July, 1941. The four crew died and there was extensive damage to property. Two bent propellers and an undercarriage leg mark the furrow dug out by an engine.

79. Men of Twineham Home Guard seem to have sensibly adopted the local pub as their H.Q.!

HORSHAM URBAN DISTRICT

In common with many towns and communities Horsham had its own "Spitfire Fund" to finance the purchase of a presentation fighter for the RAF, and its "Horsham and District Spitfire Fund" was established during the dark days of 1940 at the height of the Battle of Britain. By the early summer of 1941 over £5,000 had been raised and Spitfire W3327, carrying the name "Horsham And District", was delivered to the RAF during June. On the 25th it was allocated to 6ll Squadron at Hornchurch, with whom it served until 2lst October, 1941, when shot down four miles off Boulogne whilst on an Air Sea Rescue Escort mission. Its pilot, Pilot Officer J.F. Reeves, was presumed killed, and no trace of his body has ever been found. Ironically, the West Sussex County Times carried a picture of the Spitfire on 9th January, 1942, under the proud headline "Horsham's Spitfire - Now On Service!" In fact, it had been at the bottom of the sea for two months by the time the picture appeared! However, the public were spared such unpalatable and morale damaging facts.

Much of the credit for the Spitfire fund-raising efforts must go to Mr. W.S. Parsons, Secretary of the Fund, who worked tirelessly to achieve the goal for the presentation of Horsham's own fighter aircraft. How sad that it should have such a brief life, and that it would carry its young pilot to his death. Nevertheless, the record shows that it provided over two months of valuable active combat service with 611 Squadron, a front line fighter unit.

Only two significant air raid incidents are recorded in the Urban District for 1941. The first was on 12th January when incendiary bombs fell, and the second was on 11th June when a single bomb was dropped which failed to explode. No casualties or damage were reported in either incident and the only such episode during 1942 was on 16th December when a machine gun attack took place, again without loss of life or injury, although the High School was hit.

A tragic episode took place on the night of 27th August, 1941, when a Hurricane of No.l. Squadron crashed due to unknown causes into a cornfield at Pond Tail Lane. Sgt. Pilot Ernest Bloor abandoned his aircraft but was killed when his parachute apparently failed. The crashing fighter set fire to standing corn and today the site has become a housing development where a road is named to honour the memory of Ernest Bloor.

As mentioned in our previous volume, "*Battle Over Sussex 1940*", Horsham was home to the important HQ of No.2 Group, Royal Observer Corps, in Denne Road. Manned 24 hours a day, 365 days a year, this was a veritable nerve centre for the RAF. All outlying ROC Posts were, quite literally, the eyes and ears of the RAF and they passed details on incoming aircraft through to Horsham where the information was then relayed to an RAF Operations Centre. Supplementary to information from radar stations, the value of this visual plotting information cannot be underestimated in terms of its importance. No.2. Group, centred on Horsham, covered a significant portion of Sussex and was thus very much in the forefront of Britain's defence.

80. Karl Brunning (left) was the pilot and only survivor of a Heinkel lll shot down across the Surrey border at Ockley on 12th March, 1941. Wounded, Brunning was treated in Horsham Hospital. Unluckier were Alexander Dussel (centre left) who fell dead at Holbrook Park near Horsham. Konrad Steiger (centre right) and Willi Weisse (right) both died in the crashed Heinkel. The three were buried in Horsham, Hills Road, Cemetery.

COME AND SEE THE

HEINKEL 111

(The Giant German Bomber)

SPRINGFIELD ROAD

Near Catholic Church

MINIMUM ADMISSION 6d.   **CHILDREN 3d.**

(PLEASE GIVE MORE IF YOU ARE ABLE)

(All Proceeds to Horsham & District Spitfire Fund)

81. The Horsham & District Spitfire fund had raised sufficient (£5,000) to buy its own Spitfire for the RAF by June, 1941. This was one of the many fund raising efforts.

82. Sgt. Pilot Ernest Bloor was killed when his Hurricane fighter of No 1 Squadron, Tangmere, crashed at Pond Tail Lane on 27th August, 1941.

83. Horsham Fire Brigade became a unit of the National Fire Service and its firemen attended most of the wartime incidents in and around Horsham. They are pictured with a Bedford Fire Engine.

84. This was the Operations Centre at the HQ of No.2. Group, Royal Observer Corps, in Denne Road, Horsham. From here, the movements of all aircraft across Sussex were plotted and information passed to RAF Fighter Command. The chart details have been censored.

HOVE MUNICIPAL BOROUGH

Sporadic bombing incidents occurred at Hove during the "Blitz" period and one of the first of these was on the night of 28th/29th April when several bombs fell in the Borough. The first casualty of the period, however, was not until June, when fifteen year old Mary Priest died as bombs hit the Western Road area on the night of l3th/l4th June. Quite likely these bombs were dropped by the Heinkel lll which was the shot down by a Beaufighter, falling into the sea off the Borough with the loss of all four crew.

Later in the year an incident at Portslade Station claimed the life of a 35 year old ARP worker, Arthur Boxall, on lst October, l94l.

Incidents in 1942 were apparently confined to a minor episode on the night of l6th/l7th June and damage being caused by random bombs on the night of 9th/l0th August. In October, on 26th, the records show that 41 year old Violet May died when her home at l3 Fallowfield Close was hit. Again, it is possible that the raider inflicting this damage was itself shot down off the Sussex coast when a Junkers 88 was sent into the sea off Beachy Head by Squadron Leader "Bob" Braham, DSO,DFC.

No aircraft are recorded as having fallen in the Borough during the 1941/42 period.

85. Bob-a-Job! This was the scene in Hove on 14th June, 1941, after bombs had hit the Western Road area and Boy Scouts helped to clear the debris.

LEWES MUNICIPAL BOROUGH

An unusual local feature of Home Guard operations was the existence at Lewes of a mounted platoon of Home Guardsmen. In reality, their purpose was to patrol the South Downs but armed soldiers on horseback at the height of the invasion scare inevitably makes one contemplate the real prospect of cavalry against tanks had invasion come!

Desperate measures, however, were taken to prepare against invasion and a reminder of "last ditch" efforts came dramatically to light in the Lewes area during March, 1994, when buried "Fougasse" bombs were located in Ashcombe Lane leading from Lewes to Kingston. These devices were 50 gallon oil drums, buried in the high banks of various sunken lanes. In the event of invasion they could be detonated as enemy troops passed by, sending blazing petrol and oil cascading into the lane. Apparently, at the end of the war the twelve "bombs" buried by the Home Guard at Ashcombe Lane were forgotten and the deadly devices have

only recently come to light. - potent reminders of desperate times and reminders, too, that dangerous relics of the period still litter the countryside.

Lewes itself suffered only one civilian fatality through air raid during the period covered by this book when 77 year old Joseph Crawley died at Eastgate Street on 14th February, 1941. There were several other air raid incidents, however.

On 13th August, 1942, a Spitfire of 350 (Belgian) Squadron based at Redhill collided with electricity cables near Hamsey Railway Bridge while low flying and crashed at Lower Malling Farm, South Malling Without. The Spitfire was completely wrecked, and the Belgian Pilot, Pilot Officer De Hassey, was extremely lucky to escape with his life. Seriously injured, he was treated at the town's Victoria Hospital. Six days later, the Canadian soldiers who guarded the wreckage would be going ashore at Dieppe.

86. This was one of the improvised Home Guard "Fougasse" bombs which came to light in Ashcombe Lane on the outskirts of Lewes during March, 1994. **Filled with an inflammable mixture they were to have been detonated to entrap passing German troops in the sunken lane.**

LITTLEHAMPTON URBAN DISTRICT

A night raid on 20th/21st February, 1941, caused some damage but, thankfully, no casualties as Littlehampton experienced its first taste of the night Blitz. However, it would not be until 1942 that the town would experience any fatalities though enemy action.

In the spring of 1941, however, objects of another nature were dropped over the town - this time by the Royal Air Force. An example is reproduced of the propaganda leaflets which fluttered down over Littlehampton to a population rather more used to having German hardware falling on their heads! On 16th September, 1941, a Spitfire of 41 Squadron broke up in mid air due to structural failure of one wing, the wreckage crashing to earth and burning in a minefield at Littlehampton Golf Course. Sgt. Pilot L.Hunt was killed in this unfortunate accident which, once more, highlights the heavy toll on lives and machinery caused through accident rather than combat.

With the "Hit and Run" raids of 1942 Littlehampton's coastal position, like other seaside towns, rendered it liable to attack and, on 18th July, bombs hit Pier Road, killing seven and injuring nineteen others. Meanwhile, a convoy was attacked just offshore. On 19th August two of the fearsome Focke Wulf 190's roared in low and fast, spraying machine gun bullets across the town as they released two bombs - one of which made a direct hit on The Manse, Arundel Road. The Revd. Hailstone, his wife Hilda and Lilian Cockburn were all killed. Witnesses some distance away thought the raiders had also dropped propaganda leaflets as they watched sheets of paper fluttering gently down above the plume of smoke and brick dust which marked where The Manse had once stood. What they were seeing, however, were Hymn Sheets and sheet music which had been blasted skywards when the bomb exploded.

Ten days later there was frantic local activity with movements of troops supporting the Dieppe Raid. Overhead, masses of outgoing and incoming RAF aircraft giving air support to the operation. The proximity of Ford and Tangmere, key airfields in the operation, meant that the air was filled with aircraft. Towards the end of the operation a damaged Hurricane of 245 Squadron crashed on West Beach, Littlehampton, but its pilot, Squadron Leader Mould, was safe and taken to nearby Ford aerodrome.

A dramatic episode involving a Beaufighter of 141 Squadron happened on 25th October, 1942, when the aircraft crashed one mile NW of the town after being damaged by return fire from a Junkers 88. With his controls damaged, Pilot Officer Selman headed home for Ford but, at 900ft, the port engine caught fire whilst circling to land. Selman had no choice but to immediately make a forced landing, which he skilfully executed between the railway and River Arun just as his starboard engine failed. On hitting the ground the aircraft burst into flames but Selman and his Navigator, Sgt. Perfect, both got clear, unharmed. Perfect remained guarding the wreckage which contained highly secret radar equipment, while Selman walked to a nearby signal box and stopped the next train to Littlehampton. Riding to the station on the locomotives footplate Selman then completed his eventful journey to Ford on a "borrowed" bicycle!

The Clouds,
above Littlehampton
24th May, 1941

With Greetings and Compliments from the Royal Air Force

We have taken the liberty of dropping this upon you today for two reasons:

Firstly, it is our work to drop things about, and we love it.

Secondly, it is the first day of your War Weapons Week. During the next seven days you have the opportunity to provide the funds to allow us to drop a lot of nice little things - in other places, of course.

You are being asked to LEND, not to give your money. We will see that your money is not wasted and will give several tits for every tat.

Please do your best to back us up

87. This leaflet was dropped by RAF aircraft over Littlehampton during May, 1941, to promote War Weapons Week.

88. The aircrews of 141 Squadron, RAF Ford, pose with one of the squadron Beaufighters. On 25th October, 1942, a Beaufighter of the Squadron made a dramatic crash landing near the town.

MIDHURST RURAL DISTRICT

With the Blitz at its height the "Sunday Pictorial" of 6th April, 1941, carried a scathing and surprising full page report on Midhurst - a town they unkindly called "The Most Cock-Eyed Town in Britain". The reason for this damning piece of journalism was the refusal of the Midhurst Council to approve the installation of an air raid siren! The paper reported local feeling was that sirens disturbed their sleep, and the only concession towards warning the populace of enemy air activity were red lamps on lamp posts - too bad if one could not view a lamp post at the crucial moment and hard luck if there was an impending attack at night, because unfortunately the red lamps were too bright to be lit after dark! More than fifty years on and the scenario portrayed by the "Sunday Pictorial" seems bizarre and hilarious. If true, it does seem that the Councillors of Midhurst considered the war to be something of an inconvenient nuisance and they were most certainly not going to let it spoil the peace and tranquillity of their town. Or was this just a scurrilous piece of journalism?

On 16th July, however, the reality of war struck home with the crash of a Hurricane at Tegleaze Farm, Graffham, which resulted in the death of 26 year old Pilot Officer Antonin Velebnovsky, a Czechoslovakian pilot flying with 1 Squadron from Tangmere. Velebnovsky had flown into the top of an unseen hill at night.

On 5th May of the following year a four engine Stirling bomber plunged into a field at Gatehouse Farm, Lurgashall, after Squadron Leader Ashworth and his seven crewmen had parachuted to safety. The 218 Squadron aeroplane, returning from a raid, had apparently fallen victim to a Turbinlite Havoc and its attendant Hurricane night fighter. The Turbinlite "flying searchlight" had illuminated its target and the Hurricane closed for the kill, blasting the big bomber from the sky in mistake for a German raider! This ignominious disaster was, it seems, the only "success" attributed to the Turbinlite unit which was disbanded shortly afterwards.

The wreckage of the Stirling had hardly been cleared away when, on 18th June, a Photo Reconnaissance Spitfire struck the chimney of Gatehouse Farm and crashed into a field beyond. The pilot was killed and a fire started in the farmhouse, the occupants of which, unlike Midhurst Rural District Council, now needed no convincing that this war was dangerous!

On 9th December a Fleet Air Arm Swordfish Torpedo Bomber crashed at Harting Hill, Treyford, seriously injuring the three occupants in another flying accident which was not caused through combat or operational reasons.

The two year period covered by this book came to an end without one single fatality through enemy air attack in the district. The complacency of the Council in apparently scorning the use of air raid sirens had not been put to the ultimate test!

89. Girls of the Womens Land Army take a break from their work on the Cowdray Estate, April 1941.

90. Men of 6th Motor Coach Coy, Royal Corps of Transport, pictured at Cowdray Park during July of 1941. Civilian coaches were apparently commandeered for military use, and with warpaint covering the gaily finished bodywork of peacetime were utilised for troop transport.

91. The business end of a Turbinlite Havoc aircraft with its nose mounted flying search-light. An aircraft of this type contributed to the destruction of an RAF Stirling bomber at Gatehouse Farm, Lurgashall, on 5th May, 1942. In modern parlance, the Stirling fell victim to "friendly fire". Several Turbinlite Havoc's also crashed in Sussex. (See Aircraft Loss Tables).

NEWHAVEN URBAN DISTRICT

The story of Newhaven during the period dealt with in this book is dominated by the Dieppe Raid of August, 1942, but the town experienced its share of the war in the run-up to that now infamous day on the other side of the channel.

On 3rd/4th April, 1941, a Junkers 88 dropped four 500kg on the town from low altitude but, thankfully, none of them exploded. One bomb had its fins break off in mid air, whilst the other three buried themselves beneath tracks on the railway line. Had they exploded, disruption to the rail service would have been considerable but all three were safely dealt with by a bomb disposal squad. For this incident, two railmen were decorated for gallantly remaining at their posts throughout.

Bombs were again dropped on the night of 16th/17th April, but no significant damage seems to have been reported. However, at the end of that month the body of a German airman, Gefreiter Rudiger, was picked up from the sea off Newhaven. He had been shot down on the night of 14th/15th March; another reminder of the price paid by the Luftwaffe for its raids on the British Isles.

In July, on the 8th, yet more German fliers were picked from the sea. This time, three men were rescued from a rubber dinghy six miles offshore by the fishing vessel SM 270 "May Queen" and brought to Newhaven. Hauptmann Millahn, Unteroffizier Kraus and Oberfeldwebel Neumann were locked up at Newhaven Police Station overnight but their comrade, Oberfeldwebel Bayer, had been killed when their Heinkel lll was sent into the sea by Squadron Leader Howell in a ll8 Squadron Spitfire. On the 24th March, 1942, three bombs were dropped across the Newhaven Fort area with two of these straddling the SS *Davaar,* a "blockship" in the mouth of the harbour. Had it been sunk, then it would have prevented shipping using Newhaven port for many months and could have jeopardised "Operation Jubilee", the Dieppe Raid, in August. In this attack bombs also hit the Marine Offices and the London-Paris Hotel killing Frank Clark and Charles Gates. These were the only two air raid fatalities in the town during the 1941/42 period.

On the 1st August the military commanders must have wondered if the Germans had some prior knowledge of the Dieppe raid being planned for, on that day, Focke Wulf 190's shot up the town and hit the Fort with machine gun and cannon fire. One of the raiders, though, paid the price and Lt. Arnd Flock was shot down in his fighter-bomber off the town. His body was later picked up from the sea, but mis-identified from clothing labels as Ernst Neu under which name he was originally buried.

The raid by an Allied Commando Force on the French coast at Dieppe on the 19th August has now passed into history as one of the significant events of World War Two. Its story has been written in full in numerous publications, but it was primarily from Newhaven that the raiding force set sail and to where they returned.

The intention of the attack was to mount a "reconnaissance in force", and to capture the port and hold it for 24 hours before withdrawing. Tanks supported over 5,000 troops made up of Canadian and Royal Marine Commandos and a small force of U.S. Rangers and Inter-Allied soldiers. The raid did not exactly go according to plan, but lessons were learned which would be put to good use during the 1944 D-Day landings. It was, however, a lesson learned at a very heavy human cost; of 4,963 Canadians, only 2,120 returned to Newhaven - and many of those were severely wounded. 907 were killed, and 1,946 taken prisoner. 52 British Commandos were killed and many more wounded or taken prisoner. 550 Royal Navy casualties were suffered, which included 75 killed and 269 missing or prisoners, and the first American soldier to be killed in Europe during the war, Lieut Edwin Loustalot, U.S. Rangers. It was a terrible price to pay, and this does not include the 112 RAF aircraft lost in the operation and the 67 airmen killed or missing in what was to date the biggest single air battle of the war for the RAF.

Many airmen downed in this and other operations owed their lives to the Newhaven based High Speed Launches of the RAF Air Sea Rescue Service. At Dieppe alone, 45 airmen were saved under difficult and dangerous conditions and the rescue of British, German and American fliers from the English Channel was performed on countless other occasions by the Newhaven rescue craft throughout the war.

In no small way had Newhaven played its part in the war. However, two and a bit years of danger and action still faced the port and its town.

92. Landing craft assemble at Newhaven Harbour prior to the costly raid on Dieppe of 19th August, 1942, code named "Operation Jubilee". The landing operation was conducted primarily from Newhaven and heavy casualties were inflicted on the raiding force - particularly among the Canadian contingent.

93. Survivors of the raid, men of No.3. Commando, return to Newhaven on the afternoon of 19th August, 1942, and display the Union Flag which they briefly flew from the cliffs at Dieppe during the landing operation. Of the 5,000 troops who took part, over 1,000 were killed and more than 2,000 taken prisoner.

94. The High Speed Launches of the RAF Marine Craft Unit at Newhaven gave valuable service rescuing fliers who had been brought down in the English Channel, saving almost countless lives - Allied and German. Here, HSL 177 speeds out of Newhaven in 1942 to search for aircrew survivors of a missing bomber.

Bignor Manor in the village of Bignor was probably the most secret address in Sussex during the Second World War. Occupied by Major and Mrs Bertram the house was used as a base from where agents were sent out to Occupied Europe via RAF Tangmere. The agents, men and women of various services and nationalities, were brought down from London under strict security by Major Bertram, then serving with the Intelligence and Security Services. At Bignor Manor the agents were given final briefings and checked to make sure they carried no tell-tale evidence of having been in Britain. Very often these brave men and women would be accommodated at Bignor for some days until conditions of weather, moon or operational considerations allowed them to be taken out from Tangmere. Usually, this would be by Lysander aircraft and always at night. The cover story for these strangers being at Bignor was that they were Allied Officers who had been wounded or injured and were "convalescing". Their cover was never blown, and the normality of family life at the Manor House belied the reality of what went on there. Mrs. Bertram acted as accommodation officer for her "visitors", and saw to it that they were fed and otherwise looked after. Meanwhile, her children remained at home adding to the illusion that this was nothing other than a household doing its bit to look after and comfort our wounded Allies. Had there ever been a breach of security it could have had the most serious consequences for the Allied war effort, and there is no doubt the outward normality of life at Bignor Manor was a significant factor in preserving its secrets. Today, few passers-by would ever realise how important a place this was in the Second World War.

On the 25th June, 1941, German aircraft scattered hundreds of propaganda leaflets across the district headed " Britain is Losing the Battle of the Atlantic ". Little credence was ever attached to the content of such leaflets which, more often than not, contained misleading or untrue information. Intended to alarm and undermine civilian morale these particular leaflets did, in fact, echo the reality of a desperate situation in the North Atlantic. Thousands of tons of shipping were being sunk by U-Boats which, by now, a had a virtual stranglehold on Britain's supply lines.

During October, on the 2lst and 23rd, aeroplanes were recorded down in the district with a Tomahawk of 239 Squadron at Manor Farm, Stopham, followed by a Tiger Moth of l8 Elementary Flying Training School down at Chichester Road, Petworth. In the first incident, Pilot Officer J. Davis was killed as his fighter crashed into a meadow but Senior Aircraftman Bigginshaw (a trainee pilot) was unhurt in the Tiger Moth incident.

On the 18th November a Hurricane of 1 Squadron crashed 700 yards from Coombe Wood on the top of Bury Hill, claiming the life of Sgt. Pilot Rupple. Luckier was Sgt. Pilot Blanco, a Belgian, who escaped with a slightly injured knee when his Spitfire crashed on 8th December at Salters Farm, Sutton.

Relatively little activity of any note seems to have been recorded for the district during the early part of 1942, but on 19th August, a Spitfire of 501 Squadron returning from covering the ill-fated Dieppe raid flew into the ground in bad weather at Tolhurst Farm, Adversane, killing its pilot, 2l year old Sgt. Allan Lee. His father, a senior Police Officer at Scotland Yard, first learned of his son's death when reading a confidential regional Police report handled by his office the following day. Lee was buried with full military honours at Tangmere.

The most tragic bombing incident in the County of Sussex was that which occurred on 29th September, l942, at Petworth. It did not involve the greatest loss of life in a single raid but resulted in the deaths of 28 schoolboys, two teachers and two other civilian when Petworth Boys School was bombed by a low flying Junkers 88. Many others were injured, but the death toll could have been much higher had not some twenty other boys been at a woodworking class elsewhere in the town. Nevertheless, the scene of carnage and utter desolation was awful to behold as Police, ARP workers, soldiers, civilian and the local Rector, Revd. Harold Goodwin, clawed with bare hands at the rubble to release the dead, dying and injured. To such a small town it was a devastating blow with some families losing more than one child, or having other children injured. On the following Saturday a mass funeral was held at Petworth Parish Church, with a cortege of tiny coffins drawn up on army trucks of the Canadian Toronto Scottish Regiment and then conveyed in a sad procession to a communal grave at Billingshurst Road Cemetery. In March, 1994, a memorial was placed on the site of the school to remember those who died in this Michaelmas Day tragedy.

95. Bignor Manor, occupied by Major and Mrs. Bertram, was an important staging post for agents being taken out of or returning to Britain. These brave men and women were taken out via Tangmere at night, usually in black painted Lysander aircraft which landed in occupied France to set them down or pick them up.

The Battle of the Atlantic is being lost!

The reasons why:

1. German U-boats, German bombers and the German fleet sink and seriously damage between them every month a total of 700 000 to 1 million tons of British and allied shipping.

2. All attempts at finding a satisfactory means of defence against the German U-boats or the German bombers have failed disastrously.

3. Even President Roosevelt has openly stated that for every five ships sunk by Germany, Britain and America between them can only build two new ones. All attempts to launch a larger shipbuilding programme in America have failed.

4. Britain is no longer in a position to secure her avenues of supply. The population of Britain has to do with about half the ration that the population of Germany gets. Britain, herself, can only support 40 % of her population from her own resources in spite of the attempts made to increase the amount of land under cultivation. If the war is continued until 1942, 60 % of the population of Britain will starve!

All this means that starvation in Britain is not to be staved off. At the most it can be postponed, but whether starvation comes this year or at the beginning of next doesn't make a ha'porth of difference. Britain must starve because she is being cut off from her supplies.

Britain's losing the Battle of the Atlantic means
Britain's losing the war!

96. In contrast with the leaflet dropped by the RAF on Littlehampton, this was an example of a leaflet dropped by the Luftwaffe on Britain. This particular leaflet was scattered by the hundred across the Petworth area on 25th June, 1941.

97. This was the harrowing scene at Petworth Boys School on 29th September, 1942, as rescuers dug at the rubble with their bare hands to free the victims.

98. The view of the school from the main road as rescue work and grim searching for bodies continues. Canadian soldiers played a major part in this distressing job.

99. Petworth's darkest day. The cortege of army trucks heads down North Street bearing coffins of the victims of the school bombing.

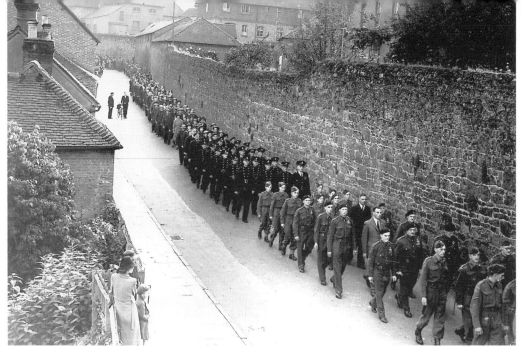

100. The funeral procession follows, en-route to the mass burial at the Billingshurst Road Cemetery. Many of those in the procession were either relatives or had taken part in efforts to free the dead, dying or injured.

101. Sgt. Pilot Allan Lee, a Spitfire pilot with 501 Squadron, was killed when his aircraft crashed at Adversane returning from the Dieppe operation on 19th August, 1942.

PORTSLADE URBAN DISTRICT

Portslade suffered lightly during air attacks although a man was injured in an incident at Portslade Station on lst October, 1941, and died the following day in hospital at Hove. (See also Hove Municipal Borough.)

Earlier in the year, on 25th/26th March, it is recorded that bombs hit the Gas Works but apparently with little effect.

On 14th April, 1942, Hitler had ordered that the air warfare being waged against England should be given a more aggressive stamp and insisted that when targets were selected only those where attacks were likely to have the greatest effect on civilian life would be chosen. Memorandum 55 672/42 went on to state: *"Besides raids on ports and industry, terror attacks of a retaliatory nature are to be carried out against towns other than London".*

This order gives some insight into the reasoning behind the attacks on civilian targets, and the raids on Sussex towns after this edict had been issued should be seen in the context of targets which had been sanctioned by Hitler himself as legitimate.

Ten days later, on the 24th, Portslade was to experience just such a "terror attack" in a daylight raid which, fortunately, caused no recorded damage or casualties.

During the years 1941 and 1942 no crashed aircraft, enemy or otherwise, are recorded within the Urban District. However, in common with the rest of the British Isles, Portslade gave of its fair share of scrap metal - even if not the product of downed aeroplanes! Indeed, plenty of evidence may still be seen in Portslade and other Sussex towns and villages of the great drive for scrap metal. In particular, ornamental iron fences and railings were cut down to help with the production of pig iron for tank manufacture. Fences from houses and factories, parks and hospitals were all removed, along with the ornamental railings which once graced many churchyard tombs. Council's attempted to get householders to donate their railings for nothing, but awkward customers were given 25/- per ton. Look around Portslade today and you will find the cut off stumps of railings in all sorts of unlikely places! How many people in generations yet to be born will realise the historical significance of these strange truncated metal stumps? Fewer still in this "disposable" society will comprehend the then urgent need for materials which gave rise to such desperate measures.

102. The removal of iron railings for the production of pig iron was carried out in towns and villages the length and breadth of Britain. Today, the cut off stumps of iron railings may still be seen across Sussex with Portslade being no exception!

RYE MUNICIPAL BOROUGH

For its small size, Rye suffered considerably during the years 1941-1942, most particularly during the "Hit and Run Raid" period. The first such episode was at 8.00 am on 15th September, 1942, when two Focke Wulf 190's hurtled in at near rooftop height from an easterly direction and released two bombs. One fell behind the famous "Mermaid Inn", bounced, and exploded in mid air. The second bomb destroyed two houses and a shop, but luckily there were no fatalities.

With the clear up operation still underway on 22nd September three Focke Wulf 190's attacked again, this time hitting the cinema killing the manager and also seriously damaging the Ship Inn, Strand House, Cinque Ports Hotel, Battery House and Ypres Tower. Three building workers from Hastings and St.Leonards were killed as they worked on damage from the previous raid.

Still shaken from these two painful attacks, the town was in for yet more special attention from the Focke Wulf 190's. This time, on 7th October 1942, a single aeroplane dropped one bomb onto a bungalow at Tram Road, Rye Harbour, killing Edith Smith and Elsie Clark.

By now the "Bofors" anti-aircraft gunners around the town (to date impotent to stop the marauding Focke Wulf 190's) were probably more than a little trigger happy. Perhaps that was the reason for the tragic event which happened on 21st October, when, at eight minutes past three in the afternoon a Beaufighter approached the town from the direction of Lydd, flying at about 500 ft. As it passed Rye Radar Station it was engaged by ground defences and nearing the town was again fired on. This time, it was hit. Smoke and flame was seen coming from the fuselage, and the aircraft banked sharply to port and crashed to earth outside the town at Watlands Farm, Udimore, killing its crew members Sgt. Wright and Sgt. Akeston of 29 Squadron, West Malling. Irony surrounds this loss, however, for earlier that day an Army Officer from Anti-Aircraft Command had lectured the crews of 29 Squadron on co-operation with AA batteries. It is thought, however, that the Beaufighter was mistaken, head on, for a not disimilar Junkers 88. Whatever, an episode such as this did little to boost the shaken morale of the townsfolk.

On the 6th December, 1942, the Focke Wulf 190's were back. This time they dropped no bombs but raked the town liberally with machine gun and cannon fire killing William Edwards on the steps near Ypres Tower. Two other civilians were hit and injured, but the Germans were gone before the anti-aircraft gunners could get an aim on the attackers.

For the bombshocked inhabitants of Rye it had been a traumatic few months.

103. This was all that remained of the Battery House in the Gun Gardens, Rye, after Focke Wulf 190's had struck on 22nd September, 1942. Four people were killed in this raid on the town.

SEAFORD URBAN DISTRICT

On 1st April, 1941, the town suffered a particularly bad attack when a single enemy aircraft released a string of bombs across Broad Street, Church Street, West Street and Chatham Place causing widespread damage. The old Manor House was destroyed and Kennards Dairy House was wrecked, killing one of the employees there, Alfred Boswell. Another bomb fell behind the Bay Hotel, almost wiping out Chatham Place and a large part of West Street as well. Near the Plough Inn a bomb had smashed through the end wall of Turrells Garage and shot across the churchyard damaging tombstones in its path - before coming to rest, unexploded, by the pub's back door just as the landlord had opened it to prove to his terrified wife that the noise outside was no cause for alarm! Considering the scale of the damage it was a miracle that the casualty toll was not higher.

On the 3rd, a Junkers 88 flew low over the town and machine gunned the area devastated in the raid two days earlier. Inevitably, there was speculation that this was the same raider who had returned to inspect his handiwork. If so, then retribution was swift. Almost immediately two Spitfires were on the scene and sent the aircraft into the sea off Seaford Head with the loss of all four crew.

Two weeks later, on Maundy Thursday, 10th April, a Heinkel 111 was shot down in flames during the late evening - the blazing bomber being a spectacle as far away as Heathfield in its final moments. By good fortune and considerable flying skill Lt. Klaus Conrad managed to put his fiery bomber down in the darkness amongst anti-invasion glider landing poles at Blatchington Golf Course - and lived to tell the tale! He held the machine steady after a devastating hail of gunfire from a Defiant nightfighter had crippled the Heinkel and, through his calmness, enabled the crew to bale out. Two landed safely, but the third, Oberfeldwebel Herman Platt, fell dead with an unopened parachute at Cradle Valley, Alfriston.

For the people of Seaford the night Blitz was, thus far, being experienced on a scale in excess of that suffered by other towns in the county and, indeed, the raiders were back on 16th April when over 1,000 incendiary bombs were scattered from Seaford Head to the Tidemills, in an attack shortly after 10pm. For a while, the whole town was illuminated by burning magnesium and phosphorus but, fortunately, little damage was done. Just to add to the terror, the enemy aircraft dropped four high explosive bombs across the scattered fires.

On the 11th May one of the night raiders, a Heinkel lll, was shot down into the sea at Cuckmere Haven. There were no survivors.

There continued to be sporadic attacks and incidents throughout the rest of 1941, but 1942 was to see the worst of the air raid incidents for Seaford.

On 9th October, 1942, there was another widespread scattering of incendiary bombs across the town when hundreds were dropped from the Cuckmere to Hindover together with eight high explosive bombs. No lives were lost, but a house in Sutton Drove was destroyed.

On the 25th of that month a low flying enemy aircraft dropped five bombs and machine gunned the town as it overflew. Broad Street, Sutton Road, East Street and Vicarage Walk were all hit and the attack resulted in the loss of twelve lives.

Not long afterwards, on 5th November, there was another raid in which Pelham Road, Dane Road, the Southdown Bus Depot and the gardens adjacent to the recreation ground were all hit and a further five civilian deaths resulted. Worthy of mention in the story of this raid is the courage of 15 year old office clerk, Betty Hamper. Betty was trapped for over six hours beneath timbers and masonry rubble but remained cheerful despite her injuries and chatted with her rescuers on the best way of releasing her. In recognition of her fortitude she was later presented with the Girl Guides Certificate of Merit for Bravery.

For its relatively small size Seaford had suffered considerably but the residents of the town had seen the worst of the attacks they would experience. Thankfully, there was no further civilian loss of life although by the end of 1942 twenty persons had died in Seaford as the result of enemy air attack.

104. This was the burnt out wreck of a Heinkel lll which landed on fire at Blatchington Golf Course, Seaford, on the night of 10th April, 1941. The pilot survived the crash landing, as did two other crew members who baled out.

105. The fourth man, Ofw. Herman Platt, fell dead with an unopened parachute at Cradle Valley, Alfriston. He was buried in Hailsham Cemetery.

SHOREHAM-BY-SEA URBAN DISTRICT

Shoreham with its harbour and aerodrome, was often the scene of considerable activity and, as may be expected, received fairly regular attention from the Luftwaffe.

Night attacks were reported on 4th/5th, 8th/9th and l6th/l7th April but it was a raid on the early hours of 9th May which badly hit the aerodrome. Three high-explosive bombs hit the buildings, setting fire to and destroying No.l. hanger but without causing any casualties. Just over an hour later two more bombs were aimed at the aerodrome and fell just to the south on open ground, one 40 and the other only 5 yards from the railway line which was blocked by debris. No doubt the burning embers of the hangar had attracted another raider to the target, but as clearance work went on yet more bombs rained down just another two hours later. This time there was a direct hit on the railway viaduct and a gas main was fractured, whilst another bomb fell just to the west of the drome and about l00 yards north of the railway. All in all, it had been an eventful night!

Despite the attentions of the German airforce, Shoreham was by no means a key defence airfield, but it did have an important role at this time as home to Air Sea Rescue Aircraft of the RAF. Lysander spotter aircraft and Walrus amphibious aeroplanes from a detached flight of 277 Squadron were based here and carried out valuable search and rescue operations over the Channel.

On 17th May, 1941, it was the turn of ships of the Merchant Navy to come under attack off Shoreham when several vessels were bombed and machine gunned by Messerschmitt 109's five miles from shore. The *SS Ala* received a direct hit on its galley, killing Rebecca Hansen, wife of one of seven Norwegian crewmen amongst the fourteen survivors taken off when the ship was beached. The *SS Arthur Wright* was damaged by blast and cannon fire, but reached Shoreham Harbour under her own steam. Meanwhile, one of the attacking aircraft was claimed as shot down by the ships anti-aircraft guns.

On the 24th May the aerodrome was again bombed and machine gunned, with bombs falling near Lancing College, The Sussex Pad, Ricardo's Works and Coombes Road. No serious damage seems to have occurred, and at least one bomb failed to explode.

The beaches of the South Coast were prohibited for access by members of the public, being festooned with defensive barbed wire, scaffolding obstructions and liberally planted with land mines. As such, they were dangerous places to be. Men of 2nd/5th Royal Welsh Fusiliers were to discover this to their cost when, on 12th September, 1941, nine of their number were killed on the beach near Shoreham Redoubt in the explosion of a mine. Only five bodies were found, and of the other four there was simply no trace.

There were similar incidents on 2nd May, 1942, and 6th May, 1942, when soldiers of Princess Patricias Canadian Light Infantry and Royal Canadian Artillery respectively were killed by land mine explosions on Shoreham beach.

On 19th August the harbour played a part in the Dieppe operation (See Newhaven Urban District) and there are records of eighteen landing craft returning to Bevis Wharf with Royal Marine Commandos, stores, prisoners and wounded men coming ashore in the aftermath of "Operation Jubilee".

Meanwhile, the work of 277 (Air Sea Rescue) Squadron continued and it was on 2nd October, 1942, that one of its most notable rescues took place. When a Lysander spotted a pilot in the sea off Cap Gris Nez, a Shoreham Walrus was despatched to rescue him. Under fire from German coastal batteries the Walrus alighted on the sea and picked up the airman despite the additional danger from mines and the risk of attack from enemy fighters. For this outstanding feat the pilot, Sgt. T. Fletcher, and his gunner, Sgt. L. Healey, were both awarded Distinguished Flying Medals.

Recorded here are but few of the numerous incidents and episodes involving Shoreham. Two more years of war would bring many many more!

106. One of the Lysander aircraft of 277 Squadron based at Shoreham for air sea rescue work. Walrus amphibious aircraft were also used, but the Lysanders function was to search for and mark the position of survivors with smoke floats which are seen under the rear fuselage. An inflatable dinghy pack is carried on the wheel spat. (Note: this photo does not appear to have been taken at Shoreham).

107. Men of the Royal Fusiliers carry out Bren Gun practice on the beach.

SOUTHWICK URBAN DISTRICT

The wartime story of Southwick is dominated by one event - the unexploded bomb at the Church of Saint Michael and All Angels.

On the night of 20th/21st February, 1941, two heavy bombs fell on Southwick - one to the south of the church and the other alongside the church tower. The first bomb exploded causing considerable damage to other property, but not to the church. The second bomb, however, had penetrated the ground adjacent to the church but failed to detonate, nevertheless causing considerable damage to the tower which cracked from top to bottom. Further damage was caused by excavation for the unexploded bomb, led by Colonel Sydney Lynn, OBE, although at first no bomb could be located. By now the tower was in a very precarious condition and the Bomb Disposal Unit consequently refused to undertake any further excavation until it had been demolished. The Ancient Monument Dept, Ministry of Works, inspected the tower in the hope of avoiding so drastic a measure as demolition, but it was ultimately decided by all concerned that there was no other safe course. It was felt, however, that such important a landmark as this tower should be preserved and it was therefore carefully taken down to the level of the ground. Every stone and each timber had been recorded on drawings and then numbered from the top of each angle quoin on each face of the tower, beginning from No.1 and continuing stone by stone, flint by flint, to the ground level. Other stones of individual features were separately recorded - such as the arcadings and small windows at the middle stages and the belfry openings at the top stage. Meanwhile, the west end of the church was supported on temporary shoring as excavations again got underway to find and neutralise the UXB. Finally, on New Years Day, 1943, a one ton bomb was discovered, de-fused and removed. It had struck downwards to a depth of about thirty feet and then taken an upward course and, until excavated, remained in a dangerous condition. Had it exploded it would most certainly have totally destroyed the church which, in 1950, had its tower restored to its former glory. This must surely be the most extraordinary and unusual set of circumstances involving an unexploded bomb in the county and could, so easily, have had a rather different outcome.

Whilst the work at the Church was underway a drama of another kind took place offshore on 23rd June, 1941, when Sgt. Pilot Beedham of 616 Squadron, Tangmere, abandoned his Spitfire after damage had been inflicted by a Messerschmitt 109 over France. Sgt. Beedham swam ashore at King Alfred Naval Station half an hour later, and was admitted to Hove General Hospital suffering from minor injuries, shock and exposure.

The following year on 12th May, George Anscombe was killed in an attack which hit the Brighton Corporation Electricity Works, whilst on 4th August three civilians were killed in a Hit and Run attack which hit Chapel Cottage, Fishergate, and 16 St. Richards Road. In the latter attack 23 year old Joyce Gatrell and her 21 month old son, Roger, were killed. Meanwhile, there were fears that the explosion of bombs in the area could cause the detonation of the bomb at the church - or else re-start its dormant time delay clock. Without doubt, those involved in dismantling the tower did so at great peril.

108. For over a year this unexploded bomb had rested beneath Southwick Parish Church and was not extracted until New Years Day, 1943. It's removal had neccesitated dismantling, stone by stone, the elegant tower. The Church was restored, post-war, to its former glory.

The Uckfield area had suffered badly from civilian loss of life during the 1940 Battle of Britain period, but when that traumatic year was over there would be no further civilian fatalities in the District until the Flying Bomb attacks of 1944. There were, however, plenty of incidents throughout 1941 and 1942.

On 18th March, 1941, Sgt. Bartlett's Hurricane of 17 Squadron crashed at Ralphs Farm, Blackboys, after he had been shot down and had abandoned his aeroplane by parachute. His colleague, Flt. Sgt. Hughes, landed by parachute at the same time in Stocklands Wood, Hadlow Down, suffering from a bullet wound to the left foot and superficial facial burns. His Hurricane crashed at Stream Mill, Chiddingly (See also Hailsham Rural district for a full account of this event).

Another Hurricane, this time flown by a Sgt. Spacek of 615 Squadron, came down at Spratsbrook Farm, Eridge, on 10th April, followed by a Defiant nightfighter crashing at Redbridge Farm, Crowborough, on the night of 17th April. From this aeroplane Flying Officer Knocker of 264 Squadron baled out with his gunner after they had been hit by our own anti-aircraft fire. (See also Cuckfield Rural District.)

On 22nd April a nightfighter of another and more unusual form crashed at Burnt Oak Farm, Jarvis Brook, killing its two crew. This was a Douglas Boston of 93 Squadron, a unit engaged in the laying of what were known as Long Aerial Mines, or "Pandoras". These were small explosive devices released on parachutes and 2,000ft of piano wire, intended to be dropped to form a curtain across an incoming bomber stream. The enemy aircraft would, in theory, fly into the wires and the explosive devices would be dragged down onto the bomber by the parachute, then detonating and crippling the raider. The scheme was not a success, and abandoned not long after the Jarvis Brook crash. This incident is said to have been the result of the pilot showing off to his girlfriend who lived locally, his exuberant and low-level "beat up" of the area resulting in tragedy.

In the early hours of 11th May, 1941, a Heinkel 111 was shot down during a night attack on London and crashed at Swifts Field in Station Road, Withyham. The bomber was blown to pieces in the crash and three crew were killed. Only one, Ltn. Martin Reiser, survived this crash.

At Park Corner, Eridge, Pilot Officer Klosin of 303 (Polish) Squadron had a lucky escape when he abandoned his Spitfire after getting into a spin from which he could not recover, adding to the tally of non-combat related aircraft losses in the county.

On the 14th of the following month, however, a Spitfire crashed at Little Bigknowle, Broad Oak, returning from an operational "sweep," Sgt. Richardson of 610 Squadron being lucky to escape his forced landing when the aeroplane ran through a hedge and overturned.

On the 31st July another return from an operations flight ended in disaster for the crew of a 142 Squadron Wellington bomber, homebound from a raid on Cologne, which crashed on Ashdown Forest at Nutley during the very early morning and caught fire. All five crew members were killed, and the remote location is now marked by a walled enclosure and a cross bearing the following inscription: "*To the glorious memory of Sgt. P.V.R. Sutton, Age 24 years, 142 Bom Sqdn R.A.F. and his five comrades who lost their lives here through enemy action 31-7-41. Mother.*"

Sutton was the second pilot, but a plaque bearing the names of his comrades has now been fixed to the wall behind the cross. This spot is often erroneously called "The Airmans Grave"; in reality it is not a grave as all of the airmen killed here are buried elsewhere.

The first aeroplane down in the District in 1942 was another Polish Spitfire, this time flown by Sgt. Warchal of 308 Squadron who was slightly injured in a forced landing at Danegate, Eridge, caused by a coolant leak on 16th April.

At 5 am on 17th June, 1942, a shattering explosion tore through the Cross-in-Hand area as a 1,000 Kg parachute mine exploded causing extensive damage but, fortunately, no casualties. Another mine drifted down at the same time to fall at Possingworth Park but this one failed to explode. This weapon, more properly called Luftmine-B, was a deadly and devastating device - particularly if it fell in a residential area where each mine was capable of laying to waste large areas.

Another Spitfire was lost in the district when,

on 26th August, Pilot Officer Lucarotti of 140 Squadron had to abandon his photo recconaisance aeroplane after his instruments had iced up. He landed safely, but his Spitfire buried itself deeply in a stream at Goldstrow Farm, Piltdown.

On 19th September another Spitfire accident claimed the life of American Pilot Officer Seymour M. Schatzberg of 133 (Eagle) Squadron, RAF. His machine broke up in mid air after a violent recovery from a dive, then crashed and burnt at Sharnden Farm, Mayfield.

The 20th December, 1942, saw the first of what would be many B-17 Flying Fortress aircraft of the USAAF downed in the county. On this day a badly shot-up aircraft of the 91st Bomb Group made it as far as Parsonage Farm, Fletching, before crash landing with no ailerons and a hole 8ft by 3ft in the tail fin. Major Bruce D.Barton put the four engined bomber named "Chief Sly" down without mishap to the crew, although Lt. Burnett had already been wounded over the target at Romilly-sur-Seine aerodrome. The record states, however, that two hapless sheep and one rabbit were killed by the crashing bomber - perhaps the only non-military loss of life through war causes in Uckfield Rural District during 1941/42!

109. Soldiers and civilians examine the battered remnants of the Heinkel III shot down by nightfighter at Withyham on the night of 11th May, 1941. The Corporal is studying a fragment of the navigators map.

110. In 1989 the wreckage of a Spitfire which crashed on 26th August, 1942, was recovered from a ditch at Goldstrow Farm, Piltdown. The engine, cockpit and fuselage had driven itself deep underground on impact.

WORTHING MUNICIPAL BOROUGH

The Borough suffered a considerable number of civilian casualties through air attack during the period covered in this book, and in total there were eighteen fatalities during the years 1941 and 1942. It was a toll not inflicted without cost to the Luftwaffe, however.

On the night of 7th/8th April, 1941, a Heinkel lll of the bomber group KG 55 was sent into the sea off Worthing by a Beaufighter of 219 Squadron crewed by Pilot Officer Hodgkinson and Sgt Dye and an incident in which all four German airmen lost their lives.

Just over a month later, on l7th May, the same pair yet again met a Heinkel of KG55 and sent it flaming to the ground at Sompting with the loss of its four crew. Two unexploded bombs were found in the wreckage and disposed of on 20th May.

In a raid on the town on lst November the Haynes Road area was badly hit, with six fatalities resulting.

The following month a Hampden bomber of 144 Squadron was just unable to make the coast and came down in the sea half a mile from Worthing Pier on 14th December.

Hit and Run raids were a feature of life at Worthing in common with other coastal towns, with attacks being experienced in April and May which caused extensive damage and loss of civilian life. However, an important feature of Britain's defence against night raiders was, by now, well and truly established in a field at Durrington. This was one of the RAF's Mobile G.C.I (Ground Controlled Interception) Stations. These were fully transportable radar stations used to track enemy raiders and to guide RAF nightfighters onto them. Durrington GCI became an important feature in the war against night bombers and the station played a key part in the destruction of many German planes brought down over Sussex.

It was also at Durrington, on 24th May, 1942, that a Vega Gull Fleet Air Arm communications aircraft came down. The pilot, Sub Lt. Churcher, was unhurt but his passengers, two Army Officers, were taken to hospital in Worthing.

On 21st July, 1942, it was a case of the rescuers becoming the rescued when a Shoreham based Walrus of 277 Squadron crashed and sank taking off from the sea 2 miles from Worthing Pier. The aeroplane was lost, but Sgts. Fletcher, Marsden and Weston were unhurt.

Probably the most dramatic aeroplane related incident in Worthing occurred on the night of 8th/9th August, l942. On this occasion a Heinkel lll, hit by anti-aircraft fire, crashed into a house at Lyndhurst Road which was then in use as a billet by men of the 3rd Anti Tank Regt. Royal Canadian Artillery. Three of the soldiers died and five injured whilst all five occupants of the Heinkel perished. The bomber had dropped high explosive and incendiary bombs before crashing, but four other unexploded bombs were found in the debris. Of greater interest to the crash investigators, however, was the curious discovery of a glider towing device in the tail of the aeroplane.

On 24th November a Tangmere based Typhoon of 486 Squadron came down at Stanhope Lodge, Durrington, slightly injuring Sgt. L. Walker in the crash landing and causing the usual local excitement among the schoolboy population who, inevitably, came to gape! There would still be excitement a-plenty for these same schoolboys across another two years of war.

111. This was the Durrington Mobile Ground Controlled Interception Radar (G.C.I.) used from 1941 to guide RAF nightfighters onto German attackers.

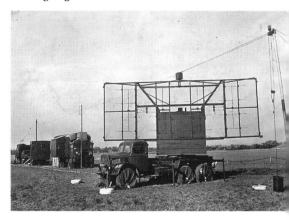

112. The severed tail sections of Heinkel lll bombers seem to have become almost commonplace during the 1941 and 1942 period in Sussex. This is the remains of one at Sompting following its loss on 17th May, 1941.

113. The four crew of the Sompting bomber were buried together at St. Mary's Churchyard, Sompting. They have since been re-buried at the Cannock Chase German Military Cemetery, Staffs.

114. This was the scene at Lyndhurst Road, Worthing, on 9th August, 1942, when a Heinkel lll had crashed into a house. Five crewmen died, along with three soldiers billeted in the house.

115. On 23rd March, 1941, this Junkers 88 was shot down by two Hurricanes at Parsons Farm, Poling, and caught fire on hitting anti glider landing poles.

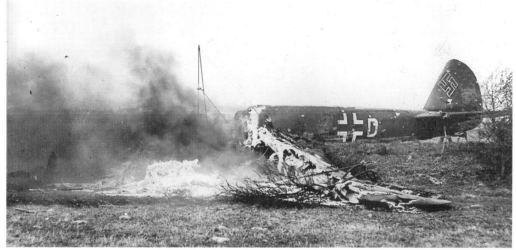

116. A close-up view of the burning wreck. The original has been signed by the two victorious RAF pilots, Flt. Lt. E. J. Morris and Sgt. F. Bernard.

WORTHING RURAL DISTRICT

One of the first incidents of note in the district was the destruction of a Junkers 88 on Sunday 23rd March, 1941, when it was shot down at lunchtime on Parsons Farm, Poling. Two Hurricanes of 238 Squadron intercepted the raider near Alton and pursued it back to the Sussex Coast where, badly damaged, it attempted to land at Poling and crashed through some anti-glider posts before coming to rest and catching fire. Three of the crew were captured, but a fourth man died. The two Hurricane pilots were Flt. Lt. Morris, a South African and Sgt. Bernard, a Czechoslovakian.

Exactly one month later, on 23rd April, another raider managed to deliver a stick of high explosive bombs on the Lancing Station and Railway Carriage Works area. At least fourteen were injured and eight houses demolished, along with the destruction of one railway coach and damage to several others. Despite all the mayhem there were no fatalities, although, as will be seen, this was not the last time the Luftwaffe would single out the Lancing Carriage Works for attention.

On 5th May, 1941, it was return fire from a Junkers 88 being pursued off the Sussex coast that crippled a Tangmere based Spitfire of 616 Squadron. Flying Officer L.H. "Buck" Casson managed to nurse his crippled fighter back to land with the intention of putting down at Ford but, as fire took hold, he was left with no option but to bale out of his Spitfire which crashed at Dover Lane, Angmering.

On 1st September a Hampden bomber of No.16 Operational Training Unit stalled in heavy mist from 300 ft and crashed at Lancing College during the early morning, resulting in the deaths of three crew. A fourth man was seriously injured.

Thankfully, during the 1941 and 1942 period there were only two civilian deaths caused by enemy action in the district; Gopal and Carmen Mulkani being killed by a direct hit on their home at Byeways, Sea Lane, on 9th March, 1941. However, the Luftwaffe returned to bomb the Railway Carriage Works on 30th September, 1942, hitting the Pullman Shed with devastating effect. Damage to building and rolling stock was severe and, in addition, 56 houses and 9 shops in the locality received varying degrees of damage. Despite the scale of the devastation there were only eighteen casualties - none of whom were seriously hurt.

For the Worthing Rural District area and the rest of Sussex it had been a gruelling and painful two years living on the receiving end of the Blitz. As 1942 drew to a close the people of Sussex had no idea how much longer their suffering would continue.

117. On 5th May, 1941, Flying Officer "Buck" Casson of 616 Squadron baled out of this Spitfire, P7753, leaving it to crash at Priors Leas, Dover Lane, Angmering, after being hit by gunfire from a Junkers 88. This picture was taken a few days beforehand at Tangmere.

118. "Buck" Casson, pilot of the Spitfire, is pictured (right) during a lighter moment at a dance in the Dome, Brighton, May, 1941. With him is Flying Officer Roy Marples who, as a Wing Commander, was killed in a mid air collision over Washington, Sussex, during 1944.

119. When German bombs hit Lancing Carriage Works
on 30th September, 1942, this was the result.

120. Another view of the Southern Railway's shattered
rolling stock at Lancing on 30th September, 1942.

AIRCRAFT LOSS TABLES

Brief details are given of each aircraft loss which the authors have on record as occurring within the county during 1941 and 1942. These listings are based upon reports contained in Civil Defence, Police and Air Ministry reports but only the basic facts are recorded here. To the best of our knowledge this is an exhaustive listing of all known aircraft crashes, although we have not shown the many such incidents on the aerodromes at Friston, Ford, Tangmere, Westhampnett, Thorney Island etc. unless they are of specific interest. As far as possible these aircraft have been listed by the administrative areas used throughout this book, although it is possible that some aircraft have been recorded in neighbouring districts where they are close to or on the boundaries of those districts, or where the records do not make it entirely clear exactly where they came down.

ARUNDEL MUNICIPAL BOROUGH

1941
NIL

1942

5. 8.1942	Spitfire	Priory Farm (collided with aircraft below)	
5. 8.1942	Spitfire	Priory Farm	
30. 8.1942	Owlet	Warningcamp Farm, Arundel	
24. 9.1942	Hurricane	Rewell Wood, Arundel	
9.10.1942	Spitfire	Bury Hill, Arundel	

BATTLE RURAL DISTRICT

1941

19. 3.1941	Hurricane	Fagg Farm, Udimore	(D86)
16. 4.1941	Hurricane	The Forelands near Broomhill	
24. 4.1941	Messerschmitt 109	Blackhouse Farm, Camber	(D87)
19. 5.1941	Hurricane	Wrens Farm, Staplecross	(D83)
28. 5.1941	Wellington	Doctors Farm, Brightling	
14. 6.1941	Heinkel 111	Lower Snailham Farm, Doleham	(D82)
18. 8.1941	Blenheim	Vane Court, Guldeford	(D80)
12.10.1941	Spitfire	Kitchenham Farm, Ashburnham	
12.10.1941	Dornier 217	Jurys Gap, Rye	(D81)

1942

24. 4.1942	Spitfire	Winchelsea Halt.	(D84)
19. 8.1942	Spitfire	Burwash	
6. 9.1942	Defiant	Whiligh, Ticehurst	
6.10.1942	Wellington	Lower Barn Farm, Salehurst	
16.10.1942	Typhoon	Netherfield	
21.10.1942	Beaufighter	Udimore	(D85)
23.10.1942	Typhoon	Ashburnham	

BEXHILL MUNICIPAL BOROUGH

1941

23. 7.1941	Spitfire	Little Common, Bexhill
27. 9.1941	Spitfire	In the sea off Bexhill

1942

2. 9 1942	Focke Wulf 109	In the sea off Bexhill

BOGNOR REGIS URBAN DISTRICT

1941

21. 7.1941	Spitfire	Oldlands Farm, Shripney
21. 7.1941	Spitfire	Marigolds Field, Shripney
23.11.1941	Spitfire	In the sea off Bognor

1942

14. 4.1942	Hampden	Sea Road, Felpham	(A26)
4. 6.1942	Hurricane	Near Bognor Gas Works	(A32)
26.10.1942	Beaufighter	The Sands, Middleton-on-sea	
16.12.1942	Dornier 217	Bognor Gas Works	(A29)

BRIGHTON COUNTY BOROUGH

1941

30. 4.1941	Beaufighter	Brighton (collided with aircraft below)
30. 4.1941	Beaufighter	Brighton
7/8.7.1941	Heinkel 111	In the sea S.W. of Brighton
19.10.1941	Havoc	Woodingdean Brighton

1942

10. 4.1942	Spitfire	The Downs N.E. Brighton
8. 5.1942	Heinkel 111	Ewes Bottom, Patcham
19. 8.1942	Spitfire	Falmer

BURGESS HILL URBAN DISTRICT
Nil

CHAILEY RURAL DISTRICT

1941

31. 1.1941	Heinkel 111	Wales Farm, Plumpton
21. 3.1941	Lysander	Balmer Farm, Lewes
5. 7.1941	Spitfire	Telscombe
16. 7.1941	Beaufort	Beddingham Hill, Lewes
8.11.1941	Spitfire	Blackbrook, Westmeston
13.12.1941	Spitfire	Owlesbury Farm, Horsted
13.12.1941	Spitfire	Broyle Lane, Ringmer

1942

14. 3.1942	Spitfire	Sedlow Wood, Westmeston
22. 5.1942	Spitfire	Stanford Buildings, Firle
25. 5.1942	Magister	Isfield Lane, Ringmer
19. 8.1942	Spitfire	Rodmell, Lewes

CHANCTONBURY RURAL DISTRICT

1941

19. 1.1941	Heinkel 111	Wyckhams Farm, Steyning	(B11)
17. 2.1941	Gypsy Comper	Pickhurst Corner, Pulborough	
20. 2.1941	Hurricane	Storrington Road, Arundel	
8. 3.1941	Hurricane	Racton Farm, Stoughton	
10. 3.1941	Spitfire	Wiston	
10. 3.1941	Oxford	West Chiltington	
31.12.1941	Magister	Amberley	

1942

4. 8.1942	Gypsy Moth	East Chiltington	
20. 9.1942	Whitley	Sullington	(B10)
15.10.1942	Spitfire	Houghton	
17.12.1942	Spitfire	Rosing Farm, Thakeham	

CHICHESTER MUNICIPAL BOROUGH

1941	1942
Nil	Nil

CHICHESTER RURAL DISTRICT

1941

2. 2.1941	Hurricane	Morrells Farm, Lagness	
8. 2.1941	Beaufighter	Gumber Farm, Slindon	
25. 2.1941	Maryland	Near Tangmere Airfield	
21. 3.1941	Beaufighter	Manor Farm, Eastergate	(A13)
23. 3.1941	Spitfire	Woodmancote	
4. 4.1941	Whitley	Eartham	
18. 4.1941	Junkers 88	Thorney Island	

3. 5.1941	Heinkel 111	Eastergate	(A27)
3. 5.1941	Heinkel 111	Sidlesham	(A28)
21. 5.1941	Spitfire	South Of Westhampnett	
21. 5.1941	Spitfire	South Of Westhampnett	(A16)
9. 7.1941	Havoc	Climping	
7. 8.1941	Hudson	Thorney Mud Flats	
19. 8.1941	Beaufort	Thorney Island	
31. 8.1941	Spitfire	Birdham	(A17)
4. 9.1941	Beaufighter	Eastergate	(A14)
7. 9.1941	Spitfire	Birdham Lock	(A18)
17. 9.1941	Beaufighter	Emsworth Channel	
26. 9.1941	Spitfire	Longford Farm, Lavant	
29. 9.1941	Hudson	Thorney Island Airfield	
5.10.1941	Spitfire	Bowley Farm	(A19)
5.10.1941	Spitfire	Sefters Farm	(A20)
10.10.1941	Magister	Barnham Court	
21.10.1941	Fairy Seal	Balsham Farm, Funtington	
28.10.1941	Beaufighter	Merston	(A15)
1.11.1941	Magister	Madehurst	
15.12.1941	Beaufighter	Fontwell	
20.12.1941	Hurricane	Adsdean	

1942

6. 1.1942	Havoc	Oughton	
16. 2.1942	Magister	West Of Tangmere	
17. 3.1942	Spitfire	Singleton	
25. 3.1942	Hurricane	West Of Ford	
10. 4.1942	Hurricane	Eastergate	(A31)
15. 4.1942	Beaufighter	Dairy Lane, Shopwhyke	(A12)
9. 5.1942	Spitfire	Oving	
22. 5.1942	Spitfire	Lavant	
5. 6.1942	Beaufighter	Boxgrove	
19. 6.1942	Spitfire	Sidlesham	(A21)
20. 6.1942	Hurricane	Little Harn Farm, Ford.	(A33)
4. 8.1942	Havoc	Little Grove Farm	(A22)
12. 8.1942	Defiant	Aldingbourne	(A34)
15. 8.1942	Mustang	Marden	
19. 8.1942	Spitfire	Stanstead Park	
19. 8.1942	Spitfire	Greenwood Farm, Sidlesham	(A30)
19. 8.1942	Junkers 88	Colworth Farm, West Dean	
28. 8.1942	Boston	Comet Corner, Middleton	(A23)
7. 9.1942	Spitfire	Lidsey	(A24)
25. 9 1942	Blackburn	Roc Near Thorney Airfield	
28. 9.1942	Spitfire	Merston	(A25)
1.10.1942	Spitfire	Near Westhampnett	
1.10.1942	Spitfire	Goodwood	
21.10.1942	Boston	Walberton)	
21.10.1942	Hurricane	Walberton) Collided	
24.10.1942	Lancaster	Wicks Farm, Ford	
3.11.1942	Mustang	Drayton	
9.11.1942	Stirling	Near Tangmere Airfield	
12.11.1942	Beaufighter	West Dean	
8.12.1942	Swordfish	Singleton	
17.12.1942	Beaufigher	Slindon	
29.12.1942	Hurricane	Tangmere Perimeter	

CUCKFIELD RURAL DISTRICT

1941

25. 4.1941	Oxford	Hurstpierpoint	
2. 6.1941	Junkers 88	Poynings	(B13)
4. 6.1941	Spitfire	Worth	
31. 8.1941	Defiant	Slaugham	
31. 8.1941	Spitfire	Devils Dyke, Poynings	(B12)
17. 9.1941	Spitfire	Twineham	
10.10.1941	Miles Master	Cuckfield.	

1942

25. 2.1942	Magister	The Old Hollow, Worth	
17. 6.1942	Spitfire	Pilstye Farm, Cuckfield	
17. 8.1942	Magister	Manor Farm, Keymer	

CUCKFIELD URBAN DISTRICT

1941
Nil

1942

19. 2.1942	Spitfire	Shepherds Hill, Haywards Heat
16.11.1942	Halifax	Great Bentley Farm, Cuckfield

EASTBOURNE COUNTY BOROUGH

1941

24. 2.1941	Spitfire	Near Eastbourne	(C

1942

20. 5.1942	Messerschmitt 109	Halfway House.	(C
19. 8.1942	Spitfire	In the sea off Beachy Head	
26. 8.1942	Focke Wulf 190	Lottbridge Drove.	(C

EAST GRINSTEAD URBAN DISTRICT

1941

5. 6.1941	Lysander	Hill Place Farm, East Grinste

1942

10. 2.1942	Tiger Moth	Holtye Road, East Grinstead

HAILSHAM RURAL DISTRICT

1941

5. 3.1941	Spitfire	Near Wilmington Airfield	(C
18. 3.1941	Hurricane	Stream Farm, Chiddingly	
19. 3.1941	Spitfire	Bodle Street	
9. 7.1941	Spitfire	Near Herstmonceux Castle	
18.10.1941	Magister	Seaford Road, West Dean.	(C

1942

27. 4.1942	Magister	Holmes Farm, Hooe	
5. 5.1942	Spitfire	Endlewick Farm, Arlington	(C
28. 5.1942	Hurricane	Litlington	(C
28. 6.1942	Spitfire	Milton Railway Crossing	(C
2. 7.1942	Hurricane	Cuckmere Haven	(C
30. 7.1942	Oxford	Ripe	
30. 7.1942	Spitfire	Parsonage Farm, Hooe	
19. 8.1942	Hurricane	East Dean	(C
19. 8.1942	Lightning P.38	Alfriston	
24. 8.1942	Spitfire	Near Ripe Church	
7.12.1942	Focke Wulf 190	Jevington	(C
17.12.1942	Spitfire	In sea, Normans Bay.	

HASTINGS COUNTY BOROUGH

1941
Nil

1942

2. 6.1942	Spitfire	Parker Road.	
2. 6.1942	Spitfire	Hoadswood Road.	
15. 7.1942	Spitfire	In the sea off Hastings	

HORSHAM RURAL DISTRICT

1941

13. 2.1941	Beaufighter	Partridge Green	
13. 3.1941	Heinkel 111	Shipley	
19. 4.1941	Junkers 88	Slinfold	
28. 7.1941	Junkers 88	Bines Road, Partridge Green	
28. 7.1941	Tomahawk	Near Ifield Post Office	
3. 8.1941	Tomahawk	Charlwood Road, Ifield	

1942

23. 4.1942	Fairey Seal	Adversane, Horsham.	
2.10.1942	Spitfire	Sights Farm, Partridge Green	
24.12.1942	Spitfire	Barns Green.	

HORSHAM URBAN DISTRICT
1941
27. 8.1941 Hurricane   Pond Tail Lane, Horsham

1942
Nil

HOVE MUNICIPAL BOROUGH
1941   **1942**
Nil   Nil

LEWES MUNICIPAL BOROUGH
1941
Nil

1942
13. 8.1942 Spitfire   Lower Malling Farm

LITTLEHAMPTON URBAN DISTRICT
1941
16. 9.1941 Spitfire   Golf Course, Littlehampton

1942
19. 8.1942 Hurricane   West Beach, Littlehampton
25.10.1942 Beaufighter   Near Littlehampton

MIDHURST RURAL DISTRICT
1941
26. 3.1941 Magister   Tillington
16. 7.1941 Hurricane   Graffham
 1.11.1941 Spitfire   Trotton

1942
 5. 5.1942 Stirling   Lurgashall
26. 5.19 42 Blenheim   Heyshott Church
18. 6.1942 Spitfire   Lurgashall
 3. 8.1942 Tomahawk   Nyewood
 9.12.1942 Swordfish   Harting Hill

NEWHAVEN URBAN DISTRICT
1941   **1942**
Nil   Nil

PETWORTH RURAL DISTRICT
1941
21.10.1941 Tomahawk   Stopham
23.10.1941 Tiger Moth   Petworth
18.11.1941 Hurricane   Bury Hill, Petworth
 8.12.1941 Spitfire   Sutton

1942
19. 8.1942 Spitfire   Tolhurst Farm, Adversane.
 4.11.1942 Lysander   Petworth
 5.11.1942 Beaufighter   Duncton

PORTSLADE URBAN DISTRICT
1941   **1942**
Nil   Nil

RYE MUNICIPAL BOROUGH
1941
26. 2.1941 Spitfire   Near Rye Harbour   (D88)
21.10.1941 Spitfire   North Rye   (D89)

1942
1. 6.1942 Junkers 88   In the sea off Rye

SEAFORD URBAN DISTRICT
1941
 3. 4.1941 Junkers 88   In the sea off Seaford
10. 4.1941 Heinkel 111   Blatchington Golf Course   (C60)
11. 5.1941 Heinkel 111   In the sea off Cuckmere Haven

1942
Nil

SHOREHAM BY SEA URBAN DISTRICT
1941   **1942**
Nil   Nil

SOUTHWICK URBAN DISTRICT
1941
23. 6.1941 Spitfire   In the sea off Southwick

1942
Nil

UCKFIELD RURAL DISTRICT
1941
18. 3.1941 Hurricane   Blackboys
10. 4.1941 Hurricane   Eridge
17. 4.1941 Defiant   Crowborough
22. 4.1941 Boston   Jarvis Brook
11. 5.1941 Heinkel 111   Withyham
 4. 6.1941 Spitfire   Park Corner, Eridge
14. 7.1941 Spitfire   Broad Oak
31. 7.1941 Wellington   Nutley
26. 9.1941 Tomahawk   Wychcross

1942
16. 4.1942 Spitfire   Rotherfield
26. 8.1942 Spitfire   Piltdown
30. 8.1942 Tomahawk   Holtye
19. 9.1942 Spitfire   Mayfield
20.12.1942 Fortress B.17   Fletching

WORTHING MUNICIPAL BOROUGH
1941
 8. 4.1941 Heinkel 111   In The Sea Off Worthing
17. 5.1941 Heinkel 111   Sompting   (B2)
11.12.1941 Hampden   Off Worthing Pier   (B5)

1942
 9. 5.1942 Heinkel 111   Lyndhurst Road, Worthing (B1)
24. 5.1942 Vega Gull   Durrington   (B7)
21. 7.1942 Walrus   Off Worthing Pier
28. 7.1942 Hurricane   In the sea off Lancing
19. 8.1942 Havoc   In the sea off Worthing
24.11.1942 Typhoon   Durrington   (B8)

WORTHING RURAL DISTRICT
1941
23. 3.1941 Junkers 88   Rustington
 5. 5.1941 Sptifire   Angmering
 4. 6.1941 Spitfire   Findoh   (B3)
 1. 9.1941 Hampden   Lancing College   (B4)

1942
31.12.1942 Boston   Kingston-on-sea   (B9)

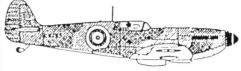